INCLUSION STRATEGIES
for Young Children

Second Edition

INCLUSION STRATEGIES
for Young Children

Second Edition

A Resource Guide for
Teachers, Child Care
Providers, and Parents

LORRAINE O. MOORE

CORWIN
A SAGE Company

For information:

Corwin
A SAGE Company
2455 Teller Road
Thousand Oaks, California 91320
(800) 233-9936
Fax: (800) 417-2466
www.corwinpress.com

SAGE Ltd.
1 Oliver's Yard
55 City Road
London EC1Y 1SP
United Kingdom

SAGE Pvt. Ltd.
B 1/I 1 Mohan Cooperative
    Industrial Area
Mathura Road, New Delhi 110 044
India

SAGE Asia-Pacific Pte. Ltd.
33 Pekin Street #02-01
Far East Square
Singapore 048763

Printed in the United States of America.

Library of Congress Cataloging-in-Publication Data

Moore, Lorraine O.
Inclusion strategies for young children: a resource guide for teachers, child care providers, and parents/Lorraine O. Moore.—2nd ed.
       p. cm.
Rev. ed. of: Inclusion strategies for working with young children.
Includes bibliographical references and index.
ISBN 978-1-4129-7107-2 (cloth)
ISBN 978-1-4129-7108-9 (pbk.)

    1. Inclusive education—United States—Handbooks, manuals, etc. 2. Children with disabilities—Education (Early childhood)—United States—Handbooks, manuals, etc. I. Moore, Lorraine O. Inclusion strategies for working with young children. II. Title.

LC1201.M66 2009
371.9′046—dc22   2008044783

This book is printed on acid-free paper.

09   10   11   12   13   10   9   8   7   6   5   4   3   2   1

Acquisitions Editor:	David Chao
Editorial Assistants:	Lesley Blake and Brynn Saito
Production Editor:	Eric Garner
Copy Editor:	Claire Larson
Typesetter:	C&M Digitals (P) Ltd.
Proofreader:	Susan Schon
Indexer:	Molly Hall
Cover Designer:	Scott Van Atta
Graphic Designer:	Karine Hovsepian

Contents

List of Figures

Preface

My interest in writing this book was inspired by the many insightful children I have worked with as a teacher and psychologist over the past years. I have shared their joy and excitement, their hopes, their disappointments, their struggles with learning, and their attempts to survive in an often harsh world. My love for children, the gratitude I have for all that they have taught me, and my desire to help create a better place in which children can learn and grow have inspired me to write this book. It is to these children, to my children John and Jane, to my grandchildren Ben and Emma, and to all children everywhere that I dedicate this book.

Acknowledgments

Corwin gratefully acknowledges the contributions of the following reviewers:

Denise Carlson
Curriculum Consultant
Heartland Area Education Agency
Johnston, IA

Christine K. Chaney
Third Grade Teacher
East Side Charter School
Wilmington, DE

Diana D. Coyl
Assistant Professor of Child Development
California State University, Chico
Chico, CA

Deborah Diffily
Associate Professor, Early Childhood Education
Annette Caldwell Simmons School of Education and Human Development
Southern Methodist University
Dallas, TX

Stacey B. Ferguson
NBCT
Multiage Teacher
North Bay Elementary School
Bay Saint Louis, MS

Deborah P. Goessling
Associate Professor, Elementary/Special Education
Providence College
Providence, RI

Denise Metiva Hernandez
M.Ed, NBCT/ECGen
Pontchartrain Elementary School
Mandeville, LA

About the Author

 Lorraine O. Moore has her doctorate in educational psychology. She has taught at the elementary and middle school levels, was a counselor in a middle school and high school, and was a school psychologist at all levels in both public and private schools. Lorraine was an instructor and adjunct associate professor in the counseling and psychology graduate education programs at the University of St. Thomas (St. Paul, Minnesota) and at St. Mary's College Graduate Center in Minneapolis, Minnesota. Lorraine has an extensive background in child development and is strongly committed to helping create more peaceful and fulfilling environments for children within a global context. She is the author of the books, *Inclusion Strategies for Young Children; Inclusion: A Practical Guide for Parents; Learning, What It Is—How Parents Can Help; Creating Balance in Children's Lives;* and *Creating Balance in Children.* Her latest book, *Creating Balance in Children's Lives,* encompasses recent research on the brain relative to its application to children's learning and well-being. Lorraine is a coauthor of the *Whole Kid Peace Activity Book.* She currently lives, works, and teaches tai chi in Madison, Wisconsin.

Introduction

Young children need to experience an environment within which they are loved and supported for who they are. They need peers of similar age with which to interact socially and to grow emotionally, so they can successfully proceed through the necessary developmental stages. **Inclusion** (this and other boldfaced words are defined in the glossary), the practice of providing programs that include children with and without special needs in the same setting, offers the best opportunity for healthy social growth and for the proper sequential development of learning skills.

This book was written for the purpose of helping adults who work with three- to seven-year-old children in school programs, early childhood settings (including preschools and day care programs), home-based programs, and other programs designed to meet the needs of young children.

Contained in this book are both guidelines and **strategies** for adults working with this age group. These can also be used for younger children who are developmentally more advanced than the average child, and for older children who are developmentally delayed in one or more areas.

The first chapter of this book outlines some *child-focused* rather than *curriculum-focused* principles for working with young children. This information can be used as a general approach to establishing best practices for working with young children or as a conceptual framework.

The second chapter provides an overview and discussion of what inclusion is and the categories of special needs and disabilities that are used with children. The remaining chapters include over 350 strategies for working with young children that cover the areas of communication, large and small **motor development**, emotional and social development, behavioral issues, preparatory writing, reading skills, math skills, and **assessment**. Sample forms that support the text are included for teachers and other adults working with young children. You are encouraged to adapt them for your situation, reproduce them, and use them as needed.

Specific reference books on a variety of topics have been recommended for developing or enlarging your resource library and expanding your awareness about working with young children. Several national organizations and Web sites are also included that you may wish to contact for continuous updated information and research.

The revised edition of *Inclusion Strategies for Young Children* provides several new strategies and an expanded resource section of books, Web sites, and organizations for all educators to access. Clarification and update of the **Individuals with Disabilities Act (IDEA)** makes this section of the revised edition more useful in understanding and working with children who have special needs. New sections appearing in this revised edition include Categories of Development, How the Brain Learns, and Mind/Body/Heart Interdependence. Educators and parents will find this new edition of *Inclusion Strategies for Young Children* an invaluable resource for working and living with children.

After considerable thought, a decision was made to use the generic pronoun "he," as it complies with standard literary practice, instead of using both "he" and "she," which can become very cumbersome for the reader. Unfortunately, until the literary community devises a neutral-gender alternative, we find ourselves in a position to take the more traditional approach for the sake of clarity and simplicity.

This book has been written with a great deal of love and compassion for children of all ages, and in recognition of all the special love and support given by the many adults who parent, provide services for, and work with young children. Through the special efforts of parents and other significant adults in children's lives a difference is made in the future of all children.

1

Working With Young Children

Children are our future. Being in a position to work with children and guide them through the maze of **learning** experiences is both a special privilege and a challenge. Success in meeting this challenge is dependent upon our love for children, our understanding of them, and the knowledge we have regarding the planning and implementation of activities that encourage their growth and development.

Information about the brain and learning has emerged very rapidly since the decade of the 1990s and continues into the present. As a result, we now have an expanded knowledge base from which we can provide a stronger support system for the development and learning of all children. Throughout this book you will find concrete ways to put into practice the necessary elements to enhance the growth and development of children by meeting their learning needs in all areas of development. To lay the foundation for putting strategies for working with young children into operation, the first part of this chapter presents a summary of some of the major findings from brain research. The second part of this chapter is devoted to child development concepts that have stood the test of time and resonate with the findings from brain research.

MAJOR FINDINGS FROM BRAIN RESEARCH

Most theorists now believe that both nature and nurture play a significant role in a child's development and ultimately who that child becomes. There is an acknowledgment that everyone comes into the world with a genetic inheritance (nature). However, it is the environment (nurture) that provides the stimuli for an individual's growth and development relative to intelligence, talents, and social abilities. The nature and nurture concept is significant information for all parents and adults who are responsible for a child's well-being and learning. The nature with which children come into the world plus the type and amount of environmental stimulation is a dynamic interaction represented by the following equation: Bf = C + E. **Behavior** (learning, social, etc.) is a function of the child and the environment.

> Behavior (physical, mental, emotional, social) = the Child + the Environment

This dynamic interaction makes it imperative that we always consider both factors when providing learning experiences for children and in planning strategies to change their behavior. The power and influence of environmental stimulation and experiences gives encouragement to adults for helping children reach their potential. It is critical that parents of young children, child care providers, and educators understand what this means and apply it to all environments where children live, play, and learn. Creating these environments is a wonderful opportunity to help children develop their potential. At the same time, it is a major responsibility to provide the environments that will support each child's growth and development. To be most effective, the timing of different types and amounts of stimuli should coincide with the child's readiness to receive it.

Children come into the world with a full set of (about 100 billion) brain cells (neurons). Stimuli from the environment are mandatory for these neurons to grow, develop, and form pathways of communication. These pathways are necessary to provide the means for language development, visual abilities, motor functions, and social and emotional growth to take place. The foundations for the development of these mind/body functions begin during the prenatal period. From birth to the first five or six years of a child's life is a critical time for the brain's neural pathways to be hardwired. Future learning and behavior are dependent upon the communications between the neurons in the brain and the cells throughout the body that are established during these early years. Young children need experiences and nurturance from adults to accomplish this important task. The richer the environment, the greater the number of interconnections are made. Consequently, learning can take place faster and with greater meaning.

In being and working with children, it is necessary to approach all we do from a mind/body/heart approach. Neuroscientists and other researchers devoted to studying the physiology of the mind/body/heart have established that these three components are interconnected and work in concert with each other. What we eat affects how we think and feel. What we think and feel affects our body's functions. In other words, cognition, emotion, and physiology are all intertwined. What we do for or to our body directly affects our ability to reason and to maintain a state of emotional balance. What happens to children (and adults) emotionally either enhances or compromises thinking ability and body functions. The body, brain, and emotions contribute to each other in complex and interdependent ways. Knowing this dynamic interplay can help adults to become more aware of ways to provide conditions and experiences that contribute to a balanced state of being rather than the less productive state of imbalance. For more information on this topic, refer to the books, *Creating Balance in Children's Lives* (Moore, 2005) and *Creating Balance in Children* (Moore & Henrikson, 2005).

Until recently, emotions were viewed from a psychological perspective consisting of both mental and feeling processes. As scientists became more adept at measuring the effect of emotions on body functions and reasoning abilities, emotions as a study moved into the circle of topics worthy of scientific enquiry. For example, scientists conducting research at the Institute of HeartMath in Boulder Creek, California, have measured the power of emotions by tuning in to heart frequencies and variability rates. They have found that the heart and the brain are constantly communicating with each other via the pathways of the nervous system to connect our thoughts, emotions, and body systems. Emotions, the physiological response of the body to external stimuli, are activated when one or more of our five senses take in information from the environment. This information is then evaluated by the brain's feeling and thinking systems to determine which response is needed. The response can vary from joy and excitement to anger and despair, which response in turn affects our cognitive and body functions either in a positive, neutral, or negative way.

In working with children, we have often underestimated the power of emotions in their lives. Emotions play a critical role in their growth and development and how they view the world around them. Positive emotional input from caring adults sets the stage to support a child's physical, mental, and social development and overall well-being. Negative input or lack of emotional support not only compromises a child's learning but puts that child at risk for viewing self, others, and the environment from a hostile or defensive perspective.

Through scientific research, nutrition has been found to have a direct link to learning and behavior. A balanced diet containing all the necessary nutrients, such as complex carbohydrates, protein, "healthy fats," vitamins, and minerals, is needed for the brain and body to support learning and appropriate behavior. Diets that consist of "fast foods," other processed foods, and sugar have been linked to poor attention, learning difficulties in academic subjects, and behaviors associated with **hyperactivity**, aggression, and depression. There has been an increase in national concern about the health of our nation's children as obesity rates and the onset of type 2 diabetes have increased among today's children. It is now a well-known fact that obesity among today's children has reached an epidemic level. The long-term consequences of obesity when the children of today become adults is yet to be determined. However, at this point we do know that type 2 diabetes can be linked to obesity, and with both obesity and diabetes come a compromised health system. Behavioral problems have also been on the increase, as observed by the increased number of children of school age on some type of medication, and with medication use extending downward to younger children. One of the more promising alternatives to medication has been to treat children by natural means such as through diet (Stordy & Nicholl, 2000). Since nutrition is now accepted as a science, more researchers are committing their time and resources to carrying this endeavor further in order to expand our knowledge of the relationship between nutrition and learning and nutrition and behavior.

Mind/body/heart research has provided us with a substantial body of updated information to help us understand and work with children more effectively. This gives practitioners a scientific basis for evaluating current child development practices to determine which practices to keep and which to change or discard. The ideas and strategies expressed in the remaining pages of this chapter and throughout the book are consistent with the mind/body/heart research.

"WHOLE CHILD" PERSPECTIVE

Children need to be viewed from a **"whole child" perspective** in order to encourage and ensure a balance in their growth and development. It is the responsibility of adults to be aware of and to address the physical, emotional, cognitive, and spiritual needs of each child. An example of what each category encompasses is shown in Figure 1.1.

If one area is overemphasized relative to other areas, children will not obtain the balance they need to develop as "whole people." Balance is critical for children to attain their full potential in all realms of life.

Figure 1.1   Categories of Development

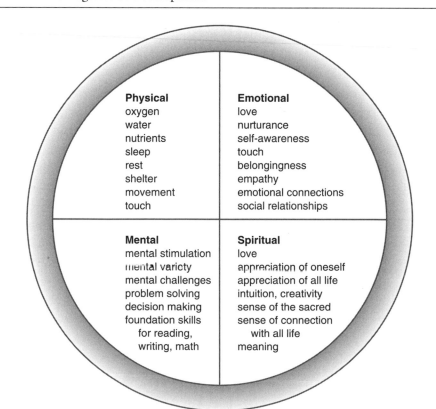

Addressing the needs of the whole child in a learning environment gives children the opportunity to optimize talents as they surface and to address their individual needs, which may be expressed as limitations. This becomes especially significant for children who experience difficulty in the learning process, as they tend to translate their areas of difficulty to all areas of their lives.

How children feel about themselves is based both upon the love and understanding they receive and upon their performance. Children with learning difficulties need to be encouraged and supported in the processes of discovering their talents and learning to use them. This allows them to develop positive feelings about themselves as people. The possibility of young children imposing the stigma of their learning difficulties universally on all areas of their lives without recognizing their talents in other areas is something that educators and parents need to recognize and prevent in order to avoid the establishment of permanently formed negative patterning.

DEVELOPMENTALLY APPROPRIATE PRACTICE

Everything we plan and do with children needs to be based on the concept referred to as **developmentally appropriate practice**. This concept is based on two principles. The first principle conveys the fact that all practices in working with children need to reflect realistic expectations for children typical of their age group. The second principle refers to the fact that practices in working with children should also be individually appropriate. Practices that are both age appropriate and individually appropriate provide the greatest opportunity for children to develop and learn at a pace that will maximize their progress. One application of these principles can be observed in curricula such as those based on the concept of differential instruction.

Development and learning are interdependent. This relationship can be implemented for each child by planning and delivering instruction and materials that fall within a child's zone of proximal development, a concept developed by L. S. Vygotsky, a Russian psychologist. According to Vygotsky, a child's level of learning and progress is determined by knowing where a child is when placed on a continuum of mastery from "can do independently" to "cannot do." This links learning to development. Expanding on Piaget's work, Vygotsky applied the concept of how social interactions and **collaboration** supported learners in the learning process. The zone of proximal development continuum appears as shown in Figure 1.2.

A child's placement on this continuum for a specific area of development is based on observation of the child's spontaneous behaviors and the child's

Figure 1.2 Zone of Proximal Development

Child does alone	Child does with assistance	Child cannot do

assisted behaviors. Informal and formal testing can supplement the observations made by the adults working with a specific child. The zone of proximal development for a particular child lies between what the child can do unassisted and what the child can do if prompted by a peer, an adult, or some other stimulus. Possible supports include interaction with the teacher, another child, or equipment and materials. All children can do more with support than they can manage alone, but the direction of growth, development, and learning is toward independence.

Another important aspect of linking learning to development is to be aware not only of where a child is in his *overall* development, but also where the child is in *each area* of development. This includes assessing where a child's language, motor, visual-motor integration, cognitive, social, and emotional abilities and adaptive behaviors lie on the developmental continuum.

It is important to remember that a profile depicting an uneven development of abilities is not uncommon for young children. This is certainly true for **children with special needs** where, in some instances, a child may be within an average range of development in one or more areas, but be significantly delayed in others.

An example of a profile of even and uneven development appears in Figure 1.3.

What constitutes a severe delay for placement into special education needs to be determined according to your school district's criteria. In most cases, age-level scores need to be translated into **standard scores** for placement

Figure 1.3 Profiles of Development

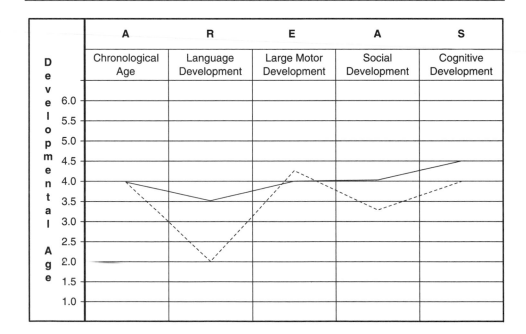

Key
—— A four-year-old boy with all areas of development within (±) six months of his chronological age
----- A four-year-old boy with a severe language delay

purposes. As a general guideline, the Gesell Institute of Human Development uses ± six months of a child's chronological age as representing development within a normal range of expectation. The Gesell Institute is an excellent source of information for understanding and measuring children's developmental ages relative to areas of development and age expectations. Their Web site can be found in Appendix B.

CYCLES OF LEARNING

The concept of **cycles of learning**, as endorsed by the National Association for the Education of Young Children and the National Association of Early Childhood Specialists in State Departments of Education, provides a foundation for learning experiences for children. According to this concept, any new learning by children (or adults) should follow a relatively predictable pattern or cycle. The cycles of learning concept is based on the assumption that a child's learning is facilitated when a four-phase, recurring cycle that begins in awareness, moves to exploration, then to inquiry, and finally to utilization is used as an instructional approach to learning.

Phase I: Awareness

In this first cycle of learning, children begin to acquire knowledge through experiencing events, objects, people, or ideas in their environment. As they process these various experiences, they develop an interest in what they see and begin to recognize some broad parameters, which they will explore in the next phase of the learning cycle.

It is the responsibility of adults to create environments for engaging children's interest by introducing them to new objects, events, and people on a regular basis. During this phase, it is important that teachers and other adults feed a child's interest by posing problems or questions, by responding to a child's curiosity or shared experience, and by displaying enthusiasm. These conditions will then give the child the impetus to move on to the next phase in the cycle of learning, that of *exploration*.

Phase II: Exploration

Exploration is the process whereby children activate all of their senses to evaluate the components or attributes of the events, objects, and people brought into their awareness in Phase I.

It is important that children construct their own personal meaning of their experiences during this time. Teachers can facilitate this by providing opportunities for active exploration, by supporting and enhancing exploration by asking open-ended questions, by respecting the child's thinking and rule systems, and by allowing for errors.

When the child has attached personal meaning to the experience and begins to draw conclusions about his experiences, it is time to move on to the third phase in the cycle of learning, that of *inquiry*. It is important to note that even though this may appear to be a linear process, in reality, children can be simultaneously engaged in two or more phases at the same time, a process of continuous spiraling.

Phase III: Inquiry

Awareness and exploration are essential but insufficient for complete understanding. A child's personal interpretations and conclusions will contain limitations imposed by the child's lack of experience and knowledge. Adults must correct and expand this thinking within the context of the child's subculture and his society. Inquiry is the process whereby children can analyze and compare their own behaviors and conclusions with what is generally accepted in a context that takes into account their developmental level.

It is the teacher's responsibility during this time to help children refine their understanding through focusing their attention, asking questions, and providing information links and other support necessary for increasing the children's understanding. The realizations and knowledge gained by children during this next phase need to be brought to the application level to fully personalize the learning and make it useful.

Phase IV: Utilization or Application

This is the functional level of learning, the stage where children can apply or make use of the learning they have acquired through the experiencing of events, objects, people, or concepts. It is at this point that the learning acquires value. It is also a point at which the learning cycle repeats itself due to the new awareness that emerges from the utilization of knowledge and understanding. As children focus on applying their learning, it becomes the teacher's responsibility to create ways for children to apply this new knowledge and understanding in a variety of situations. This phase can more easily be accomplished through a child-focused curriculum rather than one with a content focus.

To illustrate this cycle, think of the process of introducing color to children through the use of watercolor paints to create a pattern or a picture.

> *Awareness Phase:* The teacher introduces the children to the idea of exploring color through watercolor paints, by having the necessary materials set out for the children to see and having some watercolor pictures placed around the room.

> *Exploration Phase:* The teacher encourages the children to look at the materials and pictures. Given minimal directions, children then explore the concept of color by first working with one color and then progressing to mixing two or more colors together. As the children explore color through this means, they make observations about what happens when they combine colors, how the various colors make them feel, and how the colors look.

> *Inquiry Phase:* Children's observations are shared with each other. One conclusion reached is that if you mix several colors together you get brown. At

this point the teacher encourages children to share other things they have learned about color and which colors make them feel the best. It is the teacher's responsibility to clear up any incorrect conclusions and extend the children's knowledge about color appropriate for their age group.

Utilization or Application Phase: The focus for this phase is on the functional use of what the children have learned about the various colors: what happens when you mix certain colors together, how each color or combination of colors makes you feel, and so forth. For younger children, let them think about ways in which this information can be used in their everyday lives, such as the application of color in the clothes they wear and the foods they eat, how color is used in their homes, and so on.

Application of this framework can be applied to the process of learning to read, learning to write, learning mathematics, and learning any other subject matter or concept. All educators are encouraged to think about this conceptual framework in their daily work with children and to use it as a tool for analyzing and planning appropriate curricula for individuals and groups of children.

See Form 2 in Appendix A for an expansion of the format for using this approach with children.

ENVIRONMENTAL CONSIDERATIONS

The behaviors we observe and record are a result of the inner child interacting with the environmental elements of people, animals, plants, inanimate objects, and of the conditions surrounding the child's interaction. Figure 1.4 depicts this idea visually.

Behaviors (including learning behaviors) require that we pay attention to the child *and the environment* in which the learning takes place. As represented by this model, it is assumed that behavior, child, and environment are mutually and reciprocally influential. The implication of this model for meeting the needs of young children in all aspects of their development requires that we pay closer attention to the quality of children's interactions with other children and with adults in all environments and to all conditions in which these interactions take place. This model can be used to help understand children's behaviors, to determine where potential problems exist, and to plan appropriate interventions for children having difficulty in learning or behavior.

Figure 1.4   Child/Environment Interaction

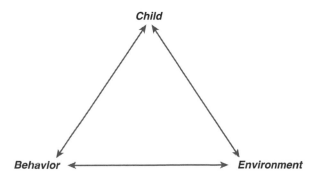

The next few paragraphs will address some environmental conditions considered significant when working with young children. Comments will be restricted to physical aspects of events and space that impact children in the environments in which learning and child care programs take place.

Events

Recognizing that children participate in several environments (such as home, neighborhood, school, day care, community, etc.), it is important to have a sense of what each of these environments is like for a particular child. For example, it is generally understood that a child carries what is going on at home wherever he goes. If the child carries love, peace, and a feeling of belonging, this will be reflected in the attitudes and feelings he carries into other situations and environments. With a positive home atmosphere, the child is better able to participate and learn in the school or day care environment.

Similarly, if a child experiences conflict, trauma, continual transition, or economic hardship, he carries the burden and impact of these events and is less likely to reach out to others and participate to his full potential in other environments. When this situation exists, the teacher or child care worker needs to play a much more significant role in the child's life in order to give him love, security, and a sense of belonging—necessary ingredients for success in learning in school.

Physical Space

The impact of lighting, color, sound, and organization of physical space on children's behavior and learning ability is being researched and is emerging as a contributing factor in a child's success or lack of success in the learning process. Adults responsible for designing and implementing programs for children need to address and apply this research.

Refer to Form 3 in Appendix A for more information on this topic.

TESTING AND LABELING OF YOUNG CHILDREN

A basic premise to remember in testing young children is that *the younger the child, the less reliable the testing results.* This is due to several factors. First is that formal tests are often based on small samples (few items) of testing behaviors. Second, the difficulty inherent in testing children due to their minimal attention span must be addressed. Third, young children may have difficulty meeting the structural demands of testing, such as being unable to understand instructions, or being unable to sit still for extended periods of time. Fourth, some children "hold back" when in the presence of a stranger. Fifth, during this growth period, young children are changing at a rapid rate, which means they are always in transition. This affects the stability of test scores over time, making them less reliable.

Due to the above conditions in the testing of young children, the labeling of various handicapping conditions needs to be done with a great deal of caution. Labeling of young children is further complicated by the fact that it is difficult to distinguish between difficulties related to developmental rate and difficulties related to organic causes. This is especially true for children who display only mild difficulties when compared to the expectations for similar age peers.

To chart a young child's progress adequately and to determine his ongoing needs, it is necessary to conduct testing more frequently than for older children. Also, a variety of tests should be used in assessing young children, including formal (standardized) tests, informal (created by the teacher) tests, observations, examples of a child's work, and parental information.

WORKING WITH PARENTS

Children are more successful in the learning process when educators and parents work together for the benefit of the child in a school or day care setting. To meet the needs of the whole child, especially those with disabilities, in a regular setting challenges our creativity for adapting curricula, developing appropriate teaching strategies, and structuring the learning environment. Success in meeting this challenge requires joint cooperation of parents and educators on a continual basis. Close collaboration on an ongoing basis between educators and parents should be a key ingredient in all settings for all children. In most cases, parents can provide the developmental background for a child, whereas educators can provide an age comparison and individual progress perspective. Both aspects are needed to provide an understanding of a child's history as well as how the child is progressing relative to similar age peers to determine if a child is growing and developing in harmony with his potential. Parents and guardians play a key role in informing educators about any current home or community-related situations and events that may impact a child's learning and behavior in the school setting. Education is a collaborative process between parents and teachers, among colleagues, and between school and community. Successfully meeting the needs of today's children is dependent upon this collaboration.

TEACHING FROM THE HEART

Children are very perceptive about how adults feel toward them. They are able to discern the difference if we tell them that we love them but do not ultimately demonstrate this love through our body language or gestures. They connect with adults through feeling rather than through the spoken word. In working with young children, it is therefore imperative that we connect with them at the heart level, allowing our teaching and interactions with them to come from the heart first, and second from the knowledge of our minds.

Recent research conducted at the Institute of HeartMath in Boulder Creek, California, has led to the discovery that the heart is vital to effective learning on all levels—mentally, physically, and emotionally. Generating feelings of love, caring, appreciation, and compassion toward young children helps reach children at the heart level to enhance their learning. These behaviors encourage children to feel, learn, and extend these behaviors to other children and adults.

When adults come from a place of love, children have a greater opportunity to self-generate feelings of love, caring, appreciation, and compassion. This, according to the research, enhances intuitive perception and increases coherence and clarity in children.

Approximately 40% of the heart's function is that of being a pump. The other major function of the heart is that of being a balancing organ that acts as an input system to the brain. This contributes to a child's emotional balance, which plays a significant role in learning and adapting to the demands of any given situation.

It is imperative that adults who work with young children understand the significance of the relationship of teaching from the heart (expressed as love and compassion) to the growth and development of children. Love, given unconditionally, is the most powerful educational tool we have. Heart intelligence, as a contributor to children's learning, is an exciting new frontier of knowledge to be explored for the benefit of all children and adults alike. To learn more about this concept and its application to working with children, visit the Web site at www.heartmath.org.

2

Inclusion

The Right to Equal Educational Experiences

All children have both similar and unique characteristics. For children who have special needs, it is important to remember that they have the same basic needs as all children. These include the physical needs for shelter, rest, and nourishment, as well as the psychological needs to be nurtured, safe, and accepted. Second, children with developmental delays and other disabilities have needs that are unique to their condition. To address the uniqueness of children with special needs requires supportive instruction, curricula, and environmental accommodations to minimize the effects of their disabilities and to promote their growth and development through the learning process.

In the past, it was felt that children with special needs could best be nurtured and serviced in environments separate from children without special needs. More recently, the practice has been to include children with special needs in the same environments that service children without special needs. Experience, research, and legislation have been the impetus to make this a reality.

This chapter will focus on the types of special needs, the legislation that supports an equal right to education for all children, and inclusive education as a concept and practice.

CHILDREN WITH SPECIAL NEEDS

The term *special needs*, in the context of this book, is used to describe children with disabilities or developmental delays. Young children are considered to have special needs when their well-being, development, and learning are compromised if not given support and accommodations to address their unique needs. The attention needed can best be provided by knowledgeable educators and child care providers who work with these children and their families in early childhood centers and school programs. Without this support, children with special needs would not make the progress for which they are capable.

In the past, children with special needs have been referred to as *exceptional* children, *handicapped* children, *special education* children, and so forth. These terms should no longer be used to refer to this group of children, as it calls attention to their disabilities, negating the fact that they are children first and foremost. It is only after recognizing their qualities as children that their disabilities should be noted. If the focus is on the disability, which implies limitation, their gifts and development as *whole people* can too easily be ignored.

Children with disabilities are generally classified by a system that defines criteria of eligibility for early intervention and special education services. To be eligible for such services under the **Individuals with Disabilities Act** (**IDEA**, formerly the Education of the Handicapped Act), children can fit into any of the categories listed as follows:

- Specific learning disability
- Speech or language impairment
- Serious emotional disturbance
- Visual impairment (including blindness)
- Hearing impairment (including deafness)
- Mental retardation
- Orthopedic impairment
- Other health impairment
- Traumatic brain injury
- Autism
- Attention deficit disorder (ADD)
- Attention deficit hyperactivity disorder (ADHD)

Because of the difficulty in detecting mild forms of disability in young children and the detrimental effects of early labeling, IDEA allows states to use the category of "developmental delay" for young children with special needs. To make this category operational, each state has specific criteria and measurement procedures for determining children's eligibility for early intervention and special education services. What constitutes a developmental delay is also included in each state's guidelines. To truly honor children, to respect the development of the whole child, and to acknowledge the tenuousness of assessing and labeling young children, it is in the best interests of all children to initially use the label of developmental delay whenever the full manifestation of a disability is not readily demonstrated.

TYPES OF SPECIAL NEEDS

Some children will be diagnosed by their physician as having specific conditions or syndromes that may meet eligibility for special services. Examples of these diagnoses include cerebral palsy, spina bifida, muscular dystrophy, and Down syndrome. It is also important to keep in mind that children exposed to cocaine, alcohol, or other dangerous substances in utero can be affected developmentally. However, the impact of these exposures can be difficult to detect at birth, as they usually surface when a child reaches early childhood or school age. For purposes of understanding the various categories of special needs, brief descriptions of the types of special needs included in IDEA are listed below:

Developmental Delay

According to IDEA, states may use this classification for young children with special needs. Each state makes its own determination as to what constitutes a developmental delay and what criteria are used to determine eligibility. Generally, to be eligible for special education services, a child needs to be significantly delayed, relative to his peer group, in one or more of the following areas of development: cognitive, physical (including vision and hearing), communication, social or emotional, and adaptive, or have a diagnosed physical or mental condition that has a high probability of resulting in a developmental delay. The category of developmental delay can be used for children from ages three to nine. However, in practice, most states use the label only for three- to six-year-olds. When a child reaches the age of seven, he is most often given the label of a specific disability such as those listed in the next several paragraphs.

Speech or Language Impairment

A speech disorder exists when a child has a difficult time correctly reproducing spoken sounds and words, smoothly producing words in sequence, and producing sounds and words within a range expected for their chronological age. When diagnosing young children's speech sounds, it is imperative to use the developmental age reference point for the emergence of each of the speech sounds.

A language disability exists when a child has difficulty expressing needs, ideas, or information compared to age expectation. This situation is often accompanied by problems in understanding language as well as the verbal expression of language. These children often get frustrated when they need to express themselves verbally, as they often know more than they can say in words. Cueing in gestures and other nonverbal behaviors is extremely important in understanding and working with these children.

Hearing Impairment

Most children with hearing impairments are diagnosed as hard of hearing rather than having a total loss of hearing. Children who have a hard-of-hearing diagnosis cannot hear the spoken word clearly, but this can often be improved with hearing aids. A young child's social behaviors and performance are almost always affected by a hearing impairment. These children need extra visual input and demonstrations to show them how to engage in and accomplish given tasks compared to the average child their age. A small percentage of children have a total hearing loss and need more specific support and accommodations.

Visual Impairment

A child who is totally blind must depend on his nonvisual senses, primarily hearing and touch, to access information. A child with even a partial visual handicap has an impairment that means, even with correction, the child's everyday performance on visually dependent tasks will be compromised. A child with partial sight has a limited ability to see print, other objects, and movement, even with correctional lenses. All written materials and visual tasks need to be adapted to accommodate these children. Since their senses other than sight tend to be more highly developed, encouragement of the use of their sense of hearing, touch, taste, and smell should be incorporated into their learning as much as possible to ensure their success.

Intellectual Impairment

Children with this disability have significantly lower intelligence for acquisition of verbal and nonverbal symbols involved in learning compared to similarly aged peers. In young children, this is often demonstrated by a slower rate of learning the skills associated with expectations for their chronological age and may appear as a developmental delay in **cognitive abilities**. This disability becomes more apparent as children engage in academic skills.

Emotional or Behavioral Disorder

A child with this disorder shows behavioral and emotional responses in a preschool or school setting that are significantly different from and often inappropriate compared to those of similarly aged peers. These behaviors or emotional responses in turn interfere to a significant extent with the child's social interactions and learning and many times to the learning of other children. Children with this disability often need therapy or counseling in addition to specific structures and expectations set up in the school environment.

Pervasive Developmental Disorder (PDD)

This disorder is characterized by severe and pervasive impairments in several areas of development. These include the areas of communication skills, social interaction skills, and sometimes the presence of stereotyped repetitive behaviors, interests, and activities. All types of PDD including PDDNOS (pervasive developmental disorder not otherwise specified) are considered a neurological disorder usually evident by age three. Some degree of intellectual impairment is often associated with PDD. Children who have this disorder generally need a considerable number of **modifications** in their instructional programs, activities, and expectations if they are to achieve success.

Autism

Autism is a developmental disability that occurs during infancy or early childhood. It is a behaviorally defined syndrome characterized by an uneven developmental profile. Most children with this diagnosis demonstrate qualitative impairments in reciprocal social interactions and with verbal and nonverbal communication. These children also tend to have a markedly restricted repertoire of interests and activities.

Repetitive, obsessive behaviors and sensory overload are problems often associated with autism. Autism is a spectrum disorder that includes mild to severe forms of associated behaviors. Less severe cases are usually diagnosed as Asperger syndrome. These children typically have adequate language skills and average to above-average intelligence but are characterized by a lack of social skills, difficulty with social relationships, poor coordination and concentration, and a restricted range of interests.

The number of students receiving services for autism has increased significantly since 1992. In 1992 fewer than 10,000 students received services, whereas by 2001 approximately 65,000 received services, according to the *Twenty-Fifth Annual Report to Congress on the Implementation of the Individuals with Disabilities Education Act.*

Traumatic Brain Injury

This term applies to open or closed head injuries caused by an external force rather than to brain injuries that are congenital or degenerative conditions or brain injuries induced by birth trauma. This type of diagnosis is made if a child's learning or social interactions are impacted to a degree of severity to warrant the need for special education and related services.

Specific Learning Disability

A **specific learning disability** is a disorder in which a child does not achieve adequately for the child's chronological age or meet state-approved grade-level standards in one or more of the defined areas when provided with learning experiences and instruction appropriate for age expectations or grade-level expectations. A specific learning disability interferes with a child's ability to acquire, organize, and express information. This can occur at the input, integration, or output levels of information. It is not due to environmental or biological factors.

Areas in which a child can be deficient include oral expression, listening comprehension, written expression, basic reading skills, reading fluency skills, reading comprehension, mathematics calculation, and mathematics problem solving.

Physical Impairment

A child with this disorder has a physical impairment that often adversely affects the child's educational performance. Examples of this disability include cerebral palsy, spina bifida, and muscular dystrophy. Physical impairments play out differently for each child in terms of ability to learn and to participate in a regular education program. If difficulties occur, individualized plans and accommodations are often needed to facilitate a child's success.

Other Health Impairment

This diagnosis refers to children who have limited strength, vitality, or alertness due to chronic or acute health problems, such as heart conditions, asthma, epilepsy, cancer, diabetes, acquired immune deficiency syndrome (AIDS), and so forth. These conditions generally result in absenteeism from school, which interferes with the child's learning progress. Special programs and schedules often need to be set up between the home and school so that these children can establish continuity in their learning.

Attention-Deficit/Hyperactivity Disorder

Attention-deficit disorder (ADD) and attention-deficit/hyperactivity disorder (ADHD) are characterized by the presence of the symptoms of inattention or inattention with hyperactivity to the degree that they interfere with a child's attending skills, performance, and self-management skills. For children to be classified as either ADD or ADHD, their inattentive behaviors or level of hyperactivity must be significantly greater compared to similar-age peers. The degree to which these symptoms exist must be measured and observed in more than one of the child's environments such as both at school and at home. The behaviors must also be present to the degree that they interfere with the child's learning performance or self-management behaviors.

IDENTIFICATION OF YOUNG CHILDREN

Labeling of young children is primarily for the purpose of determining eligibility for receiving special education services and which special education services should be provided under federal and state guidelines. It is by no means intended as a structure for curriculum and instructional purposes. Children who share the same label have a diversity of needs based on the degree of severity (from mild to profound) of their disability and the way in which their disability impacts learning and social interactions. Curriculum and instruction should therefore be based on each child's individual needs and skill development relative to how he functions in his environments. It is the specifics of a child's condition that need to be focused on rather than the label. It is imperative for educators and parents to make certain a child does not become defined by his label by clearly identifying a child's strengths, talents, and positive qualities in addition to his limitations.

Labeling of children is a challenging process, especially for younger children. For that age group, it is often difficult to determine if a delay in one or more areas of development constitutes a normal delay that will no longer be apparent by the time a child reaches third grade or if the delay continues due to a disability. To help determine this, it is imperative to know the experiential and cultural background of a child relative to his environment. Areas such as the type of experiences a child has had, the opportunities for language, emotional and social interactions, small and large motor activities, and accessibility to books are all important factors in a child's current level of knowledge and functioning. One should also take into consideration the continuity of these experiences and skill development.

Specific legal requirements for the evaluation of children with special needs are clearly stated in IDEA. *Complete IEP Guide* by Attorney Lawrence M. Siegel (see Resources Section) provides an excellent coverage of this topic.

LEGISLATION THAT SUPPORTS INCLUSIVE EDUCATION

The model most often supported by legislation, experience, and research for servicing children with special needs is inclusive education. Inclusive education, commonly referred to as *inclusion*, is defined as teaching children with special needs in the same environments as children without special needs. Inclusion allows for the needs of children with and without disabilities to have equal access to school curricula and programs. This requires that the special education teacher or consultant goes to the child in the normal school setting, rather than the child going to the special education teacher in a setting separate from other children.

There are a number of major laws regarding the concept of inclusion that have influenced the current status of special education for children age 3 through age 21 who have disabilities. However, the primary federal law that will be the focus of the next few paragraphs is the Individuals with Disabilities Education Act (IDEA). This law dates back to 1975 and was formerly known by the name Education for All Handicapped Children. In 1990 this law was reauthorized by Congress and renamed the Individuals with Disabilities Education Act. At that time the law was expanded to include the categories of autism and traumatic brain injury as recognized disabilities. IDEA was updated again in 1997 and then reauthorized by federal law in 2004. The current version of the law became effective on July 1, 2005.

IDEA as a federal law ensures services to children with disabilities throughout the nation. As such, it governs how states and public agencies provide early intervention, special education, and related services to more than 6.5 million eligible infants, toddlers, children, and youth with disabilities. State laws generally parallel IDEA and often use identical language. However, states can provide children with more, but not fewer, provisions than stated in the federal law.

IDEA supports the concept and practice of inclusive education by its language and regulations. The language used in IDEA directs school districts to place children with disabilities in the **least restrictive environment (LRE)** that meets their needs. This environment is generally interpreted as being in the regular classroom whenever possible dependent upon a child's abilities and disabilities.

In writing the law, Congress expressed a strong preference for *mainstreaming*, interpreted as placing a child with special needs in his or her classroom. To provide for a continuum of service if needed, they used the term *least restrictive environment* to ensure that individual needs would determine each individual placement. This allows for children who need a more restricted placement such as a special education class or alternative school to have that option. The determination for a child of how to best meet the needs and in what environment is the responsibility of the **individual educational plan (IEP)** team, consisting of the educators involved in the initial evaluation and the child's parent or guardian.

LRE also requires that a child be educated as close to home as possible (in the school he would attend if he did not have special needs) and to have equal access to the general curricula and programs to which other children have access. Generally this means that children with disabilities are educated in the same environment as those without disabilities.

LRE, and other disability laws not included here have become the foundation for children from birth to age 21 with special needs. It was reported by the U.S. Department of Education that all states had mandates in effect to provide free, appropriate education to preschoolers (children three through five years of age) beginning with the 1992–1993 school year. According to Wolery and Wilbers (1994), the majority of early childhood programs of various types reported enrolling at least one child with a developmental delay or disability in 1993.

The implication of these laws and state mandates is that all preschool programs, early childhood educational programs, and school programs be prepared to admit and provide services for children with special needs. Whenever possible, a model founded on the philosophy of inclusion should be used for servicing children with special needs. According to the *Twenty-Fifth Annual Report to Congress on the Implementation of the Individuals with Disabilities Education Act*, most students (about 96%) were being educated in regular school buildings, and almost half were in regular classrooms for most of the day. The remainder of this chapter will be devoted to the understanding of this model.

INCLUSION

The inclusion model for educating children with special needs looks like this:

Figure 2.1 Model of Inclusion

This model of inclusion moves away from a dualistic system of serving children with special needs that has been prevalent in public schools in the past. Implementation of the inclusion model decreases the use of "separate settings" (buildings or rooms) as places where children with special needs will be given the services they need. Instead, they receive all or most of their services in a heterogeneous setting, even though the goals for a particular child are different from those of his peers. The philosophy and practice of inclusion requires that educational systems adapt to the child rather than the child needing to adapt to the system. It is a child-focused approach to education that is clearly supported by legislation and upheld by several court decisions.

From a practical standpoint, it is important to note that the model of inclusion displayed in Figure 2.1 is based on a continuum of special education services. Recognition is first given to the rights of children with special needs to have full access to the same settings and programs as children without special needs. Second, they have a right to receive special education in these settings. Third, if all attempts to meet a child's needs in an inclusive setting do not result in success relative to an individual's learning goals, a child still has the right to more intense and differentiated services in a setting apart from his peers. This third option may need to surface for some children with severe or profound degrees of disability.

Providing a continuum of special education services conflicts with the choice made by some school districts, which have moved toward a full inclusion model. In this model, all children with disabilities receive their special education services within the regular preschool or educational setting only. For either of these forms of inclusion to be successful in meeting the needs of young children with disabilities, educators and special education teachers need to merge their experiences to work together for the benefit of all children.

Children with special needs, when placed in inclusive settings, will need modifications, adaptations, and support, just as they would if they were in a separate setting. However, the delivery system for providing these elements is different. In this instance, support is provided by a special education teacher who consults with the early childhood teacher, or a paraprofessional or special education teacher who works as a team member in the classroom. This delivery system requires that there be collaboration between professionals and parents to provide the most appropriate experiences for young children.

BENEFITS OF INCLUSIVE EDUCATION

What are the benefits of this delivery system referred to as inclusive education? There are many benefits for young children when they receive an inclusive education rather than a "separate" education. These have been documented from the experiences of educators and parents as well as from research that has been conducted over the past several years.

One of the primary benefits found for young children in inclusive settings is the increased growth in their social skills as a result of their socializing with similar age peers. From their observation and interaction with peers, they experience social behaviors appropriate for their age. This experience allows them to internalize these behaviors and demonstrate them to a greater degree than possible in separate settings.

Inclusive education promotes a better sense of belonging, a basic human need, according to Abraham Maslow's theory of psychology. Maslow pointed out that belonging is an essential and prerequisite human need that has to be met before one is able to achieve a sense of self-worth.

For some children, a degree of this sense of self-worth can come from **achievement**. For children who have difficulty learning and performing, this sense of self-worth is most often best supported by being a part of a peer group. In turn, a positive self-worth provides the motivation for a child to put forth more effort into his learning. A sense of belonging also has implications for a child's future sense of self-worth and performance in society.

Inclusive education allows a child to exercise his basic right to be educated with his peers. It emphasizes an unconditional acceptance of each child as a child, without undue focus put on his limitations. With inclusion, the child has the opportunity to participate in all facets of an early childhood or school setting rather than being fragmented into discrete parts based on needs that arise from his limitations. This provides a holistic approach to learning and a better assurance of keeping the needs of the whole child in balance.

Inclusive education minimizes the effects of labeling for the young child. This is an important benefit, as it allows greater flexibility in adjusting to the impact of maturation and development on a child's performance.

A more realistic community experience for a child with special needs is provided through inclusive settings. Through this experience, children can gain better adaptive skills. They can have more opportunities to develop friendships with normally developing peers.

Inclusive education is also beneficial for children without disabilities. It gives these children an opportunity to learn about others who are different from them, while providing them with a better representation of society as it is normally experienced.

Parents who have children both with and without disabilities have reported positive feelings about inclusion. The benefits derived from the modifications and adaptations made in inclusive settings can be used for all children to facilitate the learning process.

Communication between early childhood staff, school staff, and special education staff is increased through the practice of inclusion. Through this communication, special education staff develops a better understanding of classroom content and the typical development of children, whereas general education teachers develop a better understanding of the needs of children with disabilities. This in turn can help them better serve all students. As a result, all staff develop better ways to modify content for young children and develop reasonable expectations across all areas of learning for all children. Working together, they can also develop more efficient and effective strategies for children to use in acquiring skills. The combined expertise and resources of general education with special education programs and services maximize the learning benefits for all children.

BARRIERS TO INCLUSIVE EDUCATION

A common response to change on the part of many human beings is to resist moving into the unknown. This human trait is a barrier to the restructuring of the philosophy and belief systems that can provide appropriate learning experiences and services for young children with special needs.

A philosophical difference still exists among professionals regarding the best model for servicing young children. These differences exist among early childhood and primary grade professionals, early childhood and primary grade special education professionals, and between the two groups.

Training institutions are still predominantly educating the two groups of professionals that provide services for young children as separate groups rather than integrating common elements of both. This separation is often further compounded by inadequate training for both groups of professionals in understanding and adapting content and strategies for individual children at their local sites.

Even though inclusion as a model for meeting the needs of children with disabilities has been positive, supported by research, and backed by legislation and court decisions, there is still some reluctance on the part of some educators to move into this model. This resistance will act as a barrier until the key people delivering services to children move beyond their resistance and commit to trying something different.

Once a commitment to inclusion as a philosophy and practice for the delivery of special education programs and services is made, on-site training for all staff becomes primary for successful implementation. Insufficient staff training presents a detriment to inclusion's effectiveness.

Funding remains a continuing problem for special education services. The appropriation of funds in many instances, at both federal and state levels, has not increased in the same ratio that the need for services has increased.

The whole question of monitoring special education in private settings remains an unresolved issue. Insufficient monitoring or inappropriate monitoring of programs can hinder the success of inclusion in any setting.

SUMMARY

The benefits of inclusion will not occur without purposeful and careful support systems to promote them. For example, even though imitation is a natural way for young children to connect with an experience and learn from it, children with disabilities may not engage in this process automatically or successfully without support. They may need additional instruction from caring and trained adults. They may also need encouragement to engage in social exchanges to promote their social development and fulfill their socialization needs. Inclusion in and of itself will not guarantee that these benefits will occur.

Even though we have referred to children with special needs as a group for discussion purposes, it is imperative to remember that each child has individual needs that may be very different from a child who has a similar disability by label. The federal mandate that each child have his own IEP provides the foundation to ensure that each child receives the support, adaptations, and modifications that will facilitate his growth and development.

Training programs need to be critically evaluated for their effectiveness in preparing professionals to work with young children with disabilities in the most productive ways. Changes should be implemented as needed.

As children change and educational policies and curricula continue to change, educators and parents are being faced with new challenges. To meet these challenges, more creative approaches and collaborative efforts are necessary to fulfill the learning, social, and emotional needs of all children and especially those with disabilities. Inclusion provides individualized care to children with special needs, while forcing the learning systems to expand and be creative in order to meet these needs. When this is done, all children will benefit.

STRATEGIES

The remainder of this book will focus on strategies designed to be used with all children. In working with young children, we need to start at a child's functional or developmental level and use strategies that are the most effective for that level.

The strategies listed in the following chapters are meant to act as a springboard for the creative generation of additional strategies by the user. Children will be the happy recipients of everyone's efforts.

3

General Strategies for Working With Young Children

Many of the strategies found effective in working with children who do not have special needs can be used with children who do have special needs. These strategies should be tried first in the context of a child's experiential learning. Using this approach capitalizes on young children's concrete state of development and natural curiosity for learning.

In creating strategies, it is helpful to keep the four phases of the cycles of learning (see Chapter 1) in mind for the planning and sequencing of appropriate strategies. Observing how children engage in each of the four cycles can offer clues as to how particular children approach learning relative to how they take in and process what they see, hear, and experience. This, in turn, can provide the basis for choosing what type of strategies and how to present specific strategies for different types of learning.

The strategies listed in this chapter represent a generalized approach for working with young children. For children who have special needs, adaptations of common strategies and the creation of new strategies along with support from assistive technology communication devices may be needed.

EXPECTATIONS

1. Expectations for the performance of young children need to be based on their developmental or functional skills (what they can do) in specific areas. When a child is having difficulty performing in one or more areas, first evaluate to see if realistic expectations have been set. If not, adjust the expectations to match where the child falls functionally within the zone of proximal development (see Chapter 1) in order to apply appropriate strategies for his level of functioning.

2. Share the expectations you have for a child with his parents for each area of the child's performance in your setting. If the two sets of expectations are similar, chances are they are appropriate for the child. If not, dialogue with the parents to find the reasons for the discrepancy. Some children are also good reporters of how easy or difficult a task is for them. Make adjustments in expectations as needed.

3. Review your expectations for the child on an ongoing basis, as young children often have spurts of growth that will require periodic adjustments of those expectations. Realistic expectations allow the greatest opportunity for young children to be successful in the learning process. Setting expectations at the child's current functional levels is a prerequisite for success in the learning process.

4. In setting expectations for children who have special needs, it is important to keep the age of the child in mind as well as the functional performance level. For example, a child at the age of five who has a functional level similar to a three-year-old in a specific area needs different expectations from those of a child of three who is functioning at a three-year-old level. The five-year-old child's needs are different relative to experiences, skill development, and interests.

TIME

5. Keep in mind that young children with developmental delays or disabilities generally develop at a slower rate compared to similar age peers in their areas of limitation. However, except in the case of severe disabilities, the sequence of the acquisition of skills is similar for all children. For some children, adjusting this time factor is sufficient; for others, methods of performing the various tasks also need to be adjusted.

6. Children process information at different rates. Children with special needs often need more time to take in information, manipulate it, and respond compared to other children. Allow for this time factor in the amount of work required from the child.

7. Allow the child who processes information more slowly than other children to have extra time between your request for information and the child's response to the question (a seven-second wait time is adequate for most children).

8. Encourage other children to learn to be patient with the child who needs more response time by modeling this behavior when you interact with this type of child. This will afford the child with slower processing time a feeling of acceptance as well as providing encouragement to share his responses.

9. Be aware of a child's peak performance time during the day. Plan for the child to engage in his most difficult activity during this time if possible. This would also be the ideal time to schedule special education services if needed.

ENVIRONMENTAL CONDITIONS

10. As a part of your room arrangement, plan for a space within your room where special education teachers and paraprofessionals can work with one or more children. This space should be in the most quiet and least trafficked area of the room. Creating such a space not only facilitates cooperation among the professionals of different disciplines but also allows for a space during non-scheduled times for volunteers, support help, and other children to use.

11. Inclusive settings should be structured in such a way as to allow for small-group activity throughout the day, in addition to large-group activity as appropriate. Children with special needs generally respond better when participating in small rather than large groups.

12. Allow a few quiet areas in your room for children who need alone time as part of their day. Let the use of these areas be an option and a privilege for all children.

13. Evaluate your setting to determine the number of spatial alternatives you provide for the children. Ideally, the classroom space would allow for a broad spectrum of activity levels and styles. This includes space for creative movement, places where children can go for alone time, and social spaces for interpersonal interaction, game playing, and group projects. Arrangement and organization of space influences both the learning and behavior of children. Experiment with different arrangements and observe the effect on the children. Make adjustments to bring about an environment that will have the best impact on children's learning and behavior. Some casual furniture may also be incorporated into your space.

14. Become aware of the different background noises within the room and external to it. Work to filter out distracting stimuli by eliminating extraneous sounds if possible. Or create harmonious environmental sounds through relaxing music, recorded environmental sounds, white noise generators, or even miniature waterfalls. This will be most beneficial for the children who are sensitive to sound and for those who get easily distracted by sound. It will even act as a calmative for some.

15. Note the amount and type of lighting used in your setting. Research suggests this makes a difference in the learning and behavior of children. Full-spectrum fluorescent lighting, which contains the color spectrum indicative of natural outdoor light, has been found to support positive learning and behavior better than cool-white fluorescent lighting. Even though full-spectrum lighting is more expensive than regular fluorescent lighting, the cost is justifiable for the benefit of the children who need this consideration.

16. Color can have an influence on the learning and behavior of children. Exposing children to a wide assortment of colors and allowing them to utilize the ones that make them feel calmer and more focused have proved effective in children's performance. The choices for room colors and furniture can also have an impact on children's learning and behavior. Generally, blues and greens are more calming colors compared to reds and oranges.

17. According to Gloria DeGaetano (1993), "Preschoolers are watching more TV than ever, amassing 5,000–6,000 hours of viewing time by age 5." The rapidity of which visual, auditory, and conceptual changes occur on the screen can negatively impact children's sensory systems and sensory-motor integration. This, in turn, can impact their learning. As a teacher or child care provider, it is important to limit the use of television watching in your setting in order to provide as many hands-on experiences as possible compared to the two dimensions of the television screen.

18. Inform parents of the effects of excessive TV watching on children's learning and concentration. Encourage parents to limit their children's TV watching both in hours and in the types of programs they view.

NUTRITION AND LEARNING

19. In the past few years, more and more documentation has appeared on the relationship between diet and learning. It has been found that some children do okay with whatever they eat, while others appear to be biochemically vulnerable and reactive to refined carbohydrates, sugars, and synthetic substances that go into the body. This can result in restless behaviors, headaches, chronic fatigue, and so forth. If you observe some of these behaviors in the children you are working with, talk to their parents regarding the diet and eating habits of the child. Suggest appropriate resources if needed.

20. Nutritional deficits (caused by insufficient intake of protein, complex carbohydrates, and essential fatty acids) may result in behaviors that are commonly associated with the behaviors of children who have been identified as being hyperactive or as having learning difficulties. Consult with the parents regarding this and refer them to appropriate resources as needed.

21. Talk with your children about the importance of eating healthy foods and explain how foods affect how we feel and learn. Have children document what they eat for a given period of time and then compare their lists with recommended diets.

22. If the children you work with bring snacks or lunches to your setting, encourage them to bring only healthy food such as fruit, nuts, natural energy bars, and so on.

23. Consult with your school nurse or a nutritionist to gain information sufficient to put together a suggested list of healthy food for children to bring to school.

MULTISENSORY ACTIVITIES

24. Young children tend to use all of their senses simultaneously. When planning activities for children, incorporate as many of the five senses (sight, sound, touch, taste, and smell) as you can into each activity.

25. Plan to use movement and the involvement of the child's five senses in your activities whenever possible. This combination provides stimulation to the brain needed to develop the young child's small and large motor coordination, linguistic abilities, and body awareness.

26. For children who have sensory integration difficulties, adapt your activities to meet the needs of these children or adapt their degree of active participation in the activity. If you have access to an adaptive physical education person, physical therapist, or occupational therapist, he or she can be helpful in designing suitable programs.

BASIC CATEGORIES OF MODIFICATION

27. For children having difficulty with age-appropriate activities, reinforce the skills needed for the activity by previewing the skills needed and preteaching these skills. If the children continue having difficulty, reteach the skills required to do the same type of activity at a future time. See Form 5 in Appendix A for implementing and evaluating modifications.

28. If reinforcement does not help, try adapting the activity or the content of the activity to match the skills the child has developed.

29. If the demands of the activity or content are beyond the child's functional level at this point in time, plan a parallel activity for the child to engage in while the other children do the assigned activity.

30. Let the child participate to his degree of ability, but modify the expected outcome so the child can feel successful.

31. If a child can perform a task with adult or peer assistance, adjust the amount of assistance that the child receives, ranging from minimum to maximum assistance.

32. If it is important for a child to engage in the task other children are engaging in rather than creating a parallel activity, adjust both the task and the amount of assistance given to the child as well as the expectation.

33. Modify the steps to achieve a certain outcome for children who think in more nontraditional ways.

BRAIN BALANCING

34. Children, as well as adults, can learn and perform better if they engage the use of their whole brains. This helps to balance the functions associated with the left and right hemispheres of the brain. Using music for relaxation and doing certain types of movement activities such as brain gym activities, yoga, and tai chi can help facilitate this balance.

35. Drawing figure eights in the air helps balance both sides of the brain. To do this, have the children first draw figure eights horizontally in the air with their right hand three times. Second, repeat this using the left hand. As children are making figure eights, they are to follow their hand movements with their eyes. Then have the children use both hands going from left to right three times and then repeating from right to left three times. This activity can be done the first thing in the morning and then repeated throughout the day as desired to facilitate transitions and help children focus.

36. Refer to the book by Dennison and Dennison (1986), *Brain Gym,* for additional exercises to use for **brain balancing**.

37. Use visual, auditory, and kinesthetic input simultaneously to encourage and support the imagination of young children and to stimulate the use of the whole brain.

38. It is wise to never give up on a child. When one or more strategies do not work for a specific child, continue trying different types of strategies and modifications until some progress is observed. Some children do better when a behavior or strategy is modeled for them. Other children respond better to verbal step-by-step instructions, while others benefit from seeing the outcome before attempting to get to a specific point. See Form 4 in Appendix A for different types of strategies that can be used.

This list of strategies is just the beginning of the endless possibilities that educators in all settings and child care providers can use to nurture the mental and social development of young children. The more attention paid to this aspect of children's growth and development, the more opportunities young children have to develop and use their abilities in the learning process. When a solid foundation for learning takes place in preschool, early childhood settings, and primary school grades, children have a greater opportunity to benefit from future learning.

The next four chapters will provide specific strategies to use in the areas of communication, small and large **motor development**, emotional and social development, and management and modification of children's behaviors.

4

Communication Strategies

Communication always occurs whenever two or more people share the same space. This communication can take the form of words, body language, facial expressions, touch, gestures, or pictures, whether we are aware of them or not.

When communicating with young children, it is important to pay attention to what messages we are sending to children through each of these forms of communication. Because young children are very perceptive in observing and sensing the messages we give through nonverbal types of communication, we need to be certain the words we use are consistent with our actions. If there is a discrepancy between the two, young children will respond first to the actions and second to the words we use, or they may totally ignore the words when there is a discrepancy and act on our actions only.

To communicate effectively with children, we also need to engage as many of their senses as possible, as they tend to simultaneously use all of their senses. The degree to which we rely upon words as a communication form is dependent upon what we are communicating as well as the ability of the children to engage in verbal communication (understanding and responding). Strategies to communicate effectively with young children orally and also through the use of activities and materials will be addressed on the following pages.

BASIC COMMUNICATION STRATEGIES

Communicating and interacting with others is dependent upon having the attention of the person(s) you are communicating with and engaging in the process of listening. For young children, one or both of these basic conditions may be difficult. Consequently, the adult needs to put effort into the process of bringing about successful communication.

ATTENDING STRATEGIES

39. Secure the attention of the child with whom you wish to communicate by verbally stating or showing your need for the child to look in your direction. With younger children, you may want to use an animal or familiar character puppet to attract their attention.

40. Secure eye contact with the child with whom you wish to communicate by using words and gestures to direct the child to look at your eyes. Children of some specific cultures may not relate to a person through direct eye contact. For these children, honor their cultural tradition by emphasizing attention to an appropriate object or place.

41. Direct the child's attention to you or the object you wish the child to pay attention to by having another child or a small group of children demonstrate the appropriate attention behaviors.

42. Use sound (bell, drum, clapping of hands) while simultaneously pointing to call the child's attention to the person or object you want him to attend to.

43. Engage a child's interest in what you will be saying or doing by first approaching and participating in what the child is doing and then moving on to the place where you need the child to participate next.

44. Engage a child's interest in what you are saying or doing by using both verbal and visual stimuli to call the child's attention to your request.

45. If the child does not respond to your verbal or visual approach, use touch to engage the child.

46. When working with a group of children, scan the group to determine whether you have secured the attention of each child.

47. For children who have difficulty "tuning in" initially, have the child sit next to a child who will be a good model for him.

48. Cue the child who is not focusing his attention to where it is needed by calling attention to one or more children who are modeling the behaviors you desire.

49. Use positive affirmations to reinforce the engaging and **attending behaviors** of children who respond appropriately to your request with words such as, "I really like how Billy, Susie, and Mary are showing all of us a good way to get ready for the next activity we will be doing."

50. Reinforce appropriate engaging and attending behaviors through facial expressions (smiles are great for young children) and gestures.

51. To secure group attention at the completion of one activity and transition to the next, develop signals such as three hand claps, switching the light off briefly and then turning it back on, going to a certain place in the room, or playing appropriate music.

52. Use the element of surprise to attract children's attention such as a sudden clap of the hands.

53. Use attention-attracting phrases such as "you know what?" to engage a child's attention. A child's natural sense of curiosity makes this an effective technique.

LISTENING STRATEGIES

54. Model good listening habits for children by maintaining good eye contact (you may need to get down to the child's eye level), by hearing the child out without interrupting, and by giving feedback to show you understand the meaning of what the child is saying.

55. When working with children, note the balance or imbalance in the ratio between adult talking/listening as compared to child talking/listening. If this ratio is out of balance, make changes to bring about a better ratio. This process helps children feel valued and provides a model for talking and listening interactions. It also acknowledges their relatively short span of time for listening at younger ages.

56. Create a listening environment in the classroom by eliminating **distractions** as much as possible.

57. With children who get anxious about not being heard, assure them that each of them will have a turn at sharing.

58. Establish ground rules for listening. These may include allowing only one person to speak at a time while the others listen, looking at the person who is speaking, and so forth. Have children participate in the process of creating these ground rules as well as practicing them.

59. Provide a variety of listening experiences for children. These might include listening to music and listening to the sounds of nature. Have children identify not only the sound they hear but also the location of the sound.

60. Create a variety of listening experiences in which children close their eyes, listen carefully to what they hear and then try to make **mental images** of what they have heard. Provide a time or way (or both) for children to share what they have heard and seen mentally.

61. Speak to children in a natural voice using an appropriate volume. If a child does not hear you because he has been inappropriately noisy, do not raise the volume of your voice. Stop and wait until the child decreases his volume of noise and then proceed.

62. Adjust the pace of your speaking to allow most of the children to follow what you are saying. Encourage children to do this in their interactions with you and other children also.

63. State a purpose for listening when appropriate. This helps children listen for something rather than just looking like they are listening. This strategy helps children really "hear" what is being said.

64. In small group interactions, use the idea of a "talking stick," an object that is held by the child or adult who is speaking. Only the person holding the talking stick can speak. Others are expected to listen to that person until the talking stick is passed to another person. Start with very short periods of time and increase the time as children increase their ability to listen.

65. When communicating through the use of words, be certain the words are within the comprehension of the children with whom you are communicating. When words are out of a child's range of understanding, there is no incentive for the child to listen.

66. Encourage parents to be models for listening at home and to encourage their children to be good listeners during meal times (without the TV on) and while engaging in family activities.

67. Provide a variety of activities to encourage active listening in young children during the time they are with you. Create specific listening goals for each of these activities. Children need regular practice and appropriate modeling to become good listeners.

68. Take the time to access some of the recent magazine articles and books on developing listening skills in young children for ongoing ideas to use to facilitate active listening among children in your setting.

ATTACHING MEANING TO PRINT AND WORDS

69. Young children respond best to strategies that are an outgrowth of the context of their everyday experiences. Play, the use of toys, and engaging in tasks that are child initiated provide a wealth of opportunities for adults to promote the learning of communication skills. Utilize the experiences and objects common to children's lives for planning the strategies you can use to facilitate the development of children's communication skills in attaching meaning to print and words.

70. Children who have difficulty attaching meaning to print and words benefit from an approach called "prompting." Prompts are given by someone (usually an adult) before or as a child attempts a skill. As soon as the child learns the skill, withdraw the prompt.

71. Observe children interacting with other children, materials, and activities to determine the level of expressive communication at which each child is functioning. Use this as a reference point for developing and implementing strategies based on each child's needs.

72. Observe each child having difficulty in communicating to determine which body language, gestures, speech sounds, or words he uses to communicate what he needs or wants. Document these observations for all of the adults working with this child.

73. Plan appropriate communication goals for each child whose level of expressive language is below the expectation for the child's chronological age. Remember to develop goals that reflect the general order of expressive language development, starting from the simple to the complex, single responses to multiple responses, visual to verbal, and so on.

74. Develop a picture dictionary of common needs and experiences for children of the age group (± six months) for whom you are providing services. Have this dictionary available for children to use in communicating their needs and wants to you by finding and pointing to appropriate pictures.

75. Develop a series of visually oriented task cards that represent the sequence of steps to follow in carrying out a task. Use these task cards with children who have difficulty following a series of directions.

76. Demonstrate to all the children in your group how facial expressions, gestures, and body language act as effective, nonverbal ways to communicate with others. Then attach words describing what each of the actions mean. That way, children can experience the connection between visual, verbal, and kinesthetic communication.

77. Provide children with experiences that encourage them to use and tune in to nonverbal forms of communication. Sign language is a well-developed expressive form of nonverbal communication and one with which children are already familiar (pointing, beckoning, etc.). Sign language also helps motor development and brain hemisphere balancing, while mandating the necessity for clear communication.

78. Teach children to use pantomime as a form of communication by having them put actions to movement and then having them interpret what they saw in words.

79. Encourage both verbal and nonverbal forms of communication among children by pairing children who have difficulty expressing themselves with children who can serve as models during play and activity times when appropriate.

80. Have children communicate their needs to another child. The child who receives the message can then tell you what the message is so you can respond to the child who initiated the communication (in the manner of the familiar "telephone" game).

81. For a child with minimal expressive verbal language skills, start with a sequence of showing him an object, next showing him a picture of the object, and then naming or labeling the object. After this process, place the picture of the object in a personal dictionary for each child who needs this approach. See Form 6 in Appendix A for the steps to use in creating a personal dictionary.

82. Each day, present the child with an additional object, picture, name, or label. Add this to the child's personal dictionary. Review the other pictures in the dictionary daily by saying the name of the object and having the child locate it by pointing.

83. Perform an action for the children in your group. Show a picture of the action you have performed. Give a word label to your action. Pair the children up to take turns repeating this process.

84. Choose an action to perform for the children. Have someone find a picture that goes with the action and then label it with the appropriate words. When children become proficient at this, they can do it as a game with each other with a minimum of guidance from an adult.

85. Give a child a picture representing an action. Have the child perform the action and then label it.

86. As children begin visually to associate the appropriate word with an action or object through practice, remove the picture. Use a series of words as prompts to have children point to the word named and then describe the object or action that goes with the word.

87. Use a series of pictures to tell a story. Replace one picture at a time with the appropriate word until the story appears entirely in words. For very young children or children having difficulty with language, start out with a meaningful sentence, and ultimately work into a short story.

88. Using clay or play dough (the kind you make), have the children make their favorite animal, food, toy, and so on. Next have them draw a picture of it and then label it using inventive or actual spelling of the word. For a child with limited word knowledge or writing skills, have another child or an adult write the word for him.

89. Have children bring magazines from home. Using the pictures in the magazines, have them create their own picture dictionaries around a theme such as favorite foods to eat, favorite toys to play with, things they like to do, various expressions on people's faces, children performing different activities, and so on. As appropriate, have the child label the various pictures.

90. Choose small groups of children to create a group picture dictionary using the same procedure as listed above. In this way, children with more highly developed communication skills can be models for the children whose skills are less well developed. This process also promotes opportunities for children to interact with each other to accomplish a group task.

91. The use of rhymes and songs provides an opportunity for children to become involved in language from a whole brain perspective, which is combining the functions of the left and right hemispheres. This helps facilitate language development. It also fosters the feeling of language as well as the thinking aspects of language. Incorporate these elements into the activities of the day with young children as often as you can, but no less than twice a day.

92. Encourage each child's parents to read to their child on a daily basis. Provide a list of stories and books that are appropriate for children of the age group that you are teaching.

STRATEGIES FOR CHILDREN WITH A HEARING IMPAIRMENT

93. Consult with the professional who knows the child with a hearing impairment to learn the needs of the child. Determine the accommodations that need to be made for the child in the inclusive setting.

94. Always seat the child with a hearing difficulty near the speaker or at the center of any action involving verbal communication.

95. Use visual signals to secure the child's attention before initiating a conversation with the child, giving directions to the child, or asking the child to perform a certain task.

96. Face the child who has difficulty hearing, keeping your face within his view as much as possible, so he can read your lips and watch your facial expressions.

97. Speak and read clearly in a normal tone and at a moderate pace.

98. If a child is speaking too loudly or too softly, let him know, and then encourage him to speak within a normal range. You may have to demonstrate this for him through the use of gestures.

99. During small and large group discussions, repeat the questions and comments made, if necessary, for the child who has difficulty hearing.

100. If an interpreter is needed for a child, be aware of the positioning of that person relative to the demands of a task. For example, when a child needs to listen to the teacher, position the interpreter next to the teacher. When the child is working independently, the interpreter should be seated next to the child.

101. When communicating with children who have difficulty hearing, pair verbal communication with visual aids, such as pictures, gestures, and demonstrations.

102. Develop a series of picture cards for common directions you communicate verbally to children in your group. Pair these pictures with your verbal messages for the children who need this extra reinforcement.

103. Simplify your vocabulary, using as few words as possible to communicate a message or information to these children. An excessive use of words or the repetition of information verbally rather than by demonstration tends to overwhelm and confuse children with hearing difficulties.

104. Pair the child with a hearing impairment with a child who can model the behaviors needed for a specific task. Increase the success rate of the child with hearing difficulties by having him replicate the actions that are being modeled for task completion.

105. Make drawings or photographs of the steps for multiple-step activities. Keep these pictures on file for children to use as visual aids when needed to perform a specific activity.

106. When giving directions to a child with a hearing impairment, have the child repeat the directions back to you or to a peer to check for understanding.

107. For the child who has a hearing impairment, appoint a peer to cue the child when oral direction or information is given. Check for understanding as needed.

STRATEGIES FOR CHILDREN
WITH A VISUAL IMPAIRMENT

108. Consult with the teacher or agency that is knowledgeable about the child who has a visual impairment to determine the child's needs relative to participating in an inclusion program.

109. Optical aids, such as enlargers or magnifiers, can be very helpful for children who are partially sighted. The use of these is dependent upon the child's degree of disability and the visual demands of the task. If there are any questions regarding the use of these, it is best to consult with someone who is trained in working with children who have a visual impairment.

110. If you use supplemental devices for one or more children in your setting, take the time to describe the devices (how they are used and why) to the other children in your group. This will help both the individual child and the other children to feel a part of the total group and also to learn about individual differences.

111. Lighting, both the angle and intensity, is very important for the child who has difficulty seeing. Evaluate the lighting under which the child does his tasks to determine the most effective situation for the child.

112. Allow the child extra time to complete his tasks, if needed. Be aware of visual fatigue during activities requiring continuous use of visual skills. Some signs of visual fatigue may include red eyes, rubbing of the eyes, laying the head down on the workspace, and squinting.

113. Minimize fatigue for the child by modifying the number and length of activities that require visual concentration. For this child, keep in mind the number of repetitions needed for mastery rather than completing a specified number for a particular assignment.

114. When conversing with a child who has difficulty seeing, always address the child by name to help him cue into the interaction between the two of you. Also encourage the other children in your group to use this strategy.

115. Whenever possible, to decrease the risk of visual fatigue, parallel the visual activity with auditory input. Instruct the child to make mental pictures in his head while listening. Then have the child share these images with a peer or adult rather than writing his thoughts on paper.

116. Touch is very important for children who have a visual impairment. Provide these children with as many tactile experiences as possible to help connect with learning experiences.

117. For some children, colors placed over visual stimuli, such as pictures and print, help to enhance the contrast and darken the print so the visual demands on them decrease. Experiment with a yellow acetate overlay and with other colors to see which is the most effective.

118. When appropriate, use black marking pens to trace over print and pictures on the material used by children with dimmed vision. This helps to darken the print for them, making fewer demands on them visually.

119. Children with impaired vision need to have as much contrast as possible between the color of the print and the color of the paper. For example, black ink on white paper provides a good contrast. Colored paper and light colored inks may not give a sufficient contrast.

120. Utilize the child's sensory systems of touch, smell, and hearing as much as possible when communicating with children who have less highly developed sight. This helps reduce the demands on the child's sight and also teaches the child to use other sensory systems in communicating with others.

STRATEGIES AND INFORMATION FOR CHILDREN WITH LIMITED SPEECH AND EXPRESSIVE LANGUAGE

Many of the strategies listed above can be used effectively with children who have limited speech and expressive language. In addition, there are new assistive technologies available to use with this group of children. Such technologies, which exist in the form of devices and aids, enable children to be more independent in inclusive environments and to benefit from services provided by professionals. In many cases, both devices and strategies are needed for effective communication. Currently, there are two basic types of aids or technologies in use.

Direct Selection Aids

A technique or aid in which vocabulary takes the form of objects, pictures, symbols, or letters and words is known as a direct selection aid. To access this information, the child directly indicates his choice by using a finger, hand, eye gaze, pointer, or other means. Examples of this type include communication boards, communication vests, and E-trans devices. See Parette, Dunn, & Hoge (1995), "Low-cost communication devices for children with disabilities and their family members," for additional information on these devices.

Scanning Aids

These consist of any technique or aid in which vocabulary items are offered to the child visually or auditorily and the child makes his choice by responding, usually with some type of switch. Examples of this type of device are the loop tapes (auditory-scanning voice output communication devices), communication clocks, compartmentalized communicators, and sequential scanners.

121. A variety of resources exist to assist child care providers and teachers in their efforts to achieve compliance with the Americans with Disabilities Act. To access these, call the American Speech-Language-Hearing Association (800-638-8255) to obtain information regarding auxiliary aids and services if there is no special education professional available. For information specific to a particular child, work with the local school district's speech and language pathologist, who has expertise in augmentative and alternative communication.

ASSISTIVE TECHNOLOGY

There are a variety of assistive technology devices that are available for children to help them with everyday communication activities.

Tools for children with learning disabilities and other handicapping conditions such as visual impairment can be as simple as highlighters, color-coded files or drawers, audiobooks, tape recorders, calculators, or a different paper color or background color on a computer screen. Complex or high-tech assistive technology devices include

- computers with print-recognition software that "read" text aloud,
- speech recognition systems that turn oral language into written text, and
- talking calculators that assist people with math difficulties.

In general, assistive technology can help children who need extra support to become more independent learners. It can also help them improve their speed and accuracy of work. However, assistive technology is not meant to replace intentional, well-designed, and implemented instruction.

There are many sources of information about assistive technology. One place to start gaining more information is to contact the Schwab Learning Center (see Appendix B) to download their *Assistive Technology Guide–3rd Edition.* This guide is free.

Effective communication is critical in the lives and learning of children. New ways of accessing information and new ways of effectively interacting with one another will continue to challenge our creativity and ingeniousness. This chapter represents only the beginning of such an endeavor.

5

Large and Small Motor Development

Development of motor skills plays an important part in a child's physical development, social development, and learning. Large motor development encompasses the movement of large muscle groups, such as arms and legs, and precedes small (fine) motor development, which involves the use of hands and fingers. Since most motor activities have a visual component, a child's success in using his motor skills is also dependent upon his eye-hand coordination, referred to as **visual-motor integration**.

All children basically follow the same sequence of growth and development, but do so at different rates. Children with developmental delays and other identified disabilities often develop at a slower rate than their peers. The strategies in this chapter can be adjusted and modified to fit the needs of most children.

STRATEGIES FOR LARGE MOTOR DEVELOPMENT

Children will be at different levels in their mastery of the basic forms of locomotion, such as running, galloping, hopping, skipping, and so forth. If any children are significantly discrepant from their age expectation, make note of this and then chart their progress over the first few months of your program. If you see no improvement in skills relative to their initial reference point, consult with personnel from your local school district's special education department. In many school districts, this would be the adaptive physical education teacher.

122. Incorporate all the attributes of movement you can whenever you are planning large motor activities for children. These attributes include coordination, agility, balance, flexibility, strength, speed, and endurance.

123. Have children develop balance by providing a six-foot string or yarn stretched into a straight line on the floor. Let children practice their balance by taking turns walking on the line while placing one foot in front of the other.

124. As children gain their balance walking a six-foot line, have them increase their balancing skills by carrying various objects, first in one hand, then in the other, and then in both hands. Varying the size, weight, and shape of the objects will further improve their skills.

125. Using a six-foot string, create different shapes such as a circle, ellipse, figure eight, and so on to add interest and flexibility to the task of practicing balance by walking the pattern of the various shapes. Designing more complex shapes such as labyrinths (mazes) can be even more interesting and more challenging.

126. Children need practice throwing and catching objects. These exercises can and should be adapted so that each child experiences success in doing them. For example, in catching and throwing beanbags, some children may need to stand still and throw their beanbag gently into the air in order to catch them. Others can walk while tossing their beanbags into the air and catching them. Others can toss their beanbags back and forth to partners or among a group of children, while others with severe difficulties may have to stand with their hands forming a bowl and learn to grasp the beanbag that an adult or another child gently throws towards them.

127. When children are bursting with energy, they require motor activity as an outlet. It is important to allow them to fulfill their need for motor activity several times a day. Some of this can be during free activity time organized in conjunction with a playground or designated space within a building.

128. Add music to physical activities. Children can move to the rhythm of music spontaneously or in a planned sequence. Moving to music supports the development of motor abilities and often makes it more fun for the less physically involved children. It also helps them to move more freely by developing patterns of movement.

129. Simple dances are excellent for children in that they combine a number of skills such as listening, following directions, large muscle exercise, body awareness, and moving in repetitive patterns.

130. Provide children with large blocks of many different shapes and sizes. With these they can be encouraged to build structures, roads, model cars, and so forth, which will help them see the relationship between objects and space. This is an important concept to teach children: that movement always has some relationship to space.

131. Give the children a variety of large toys that require the children to use their large muscle groups to manipulate.

132. Different movements of the arms and legs can be combined with walking. For example, have children practice moving the right arm simultaneously with the right leg and the left arm with the left leg while they walk. Then have the children step forward with the left leg while simultaneously moving the right arm forward; right leg forward, left arm forward, and so on. These movements can also be done in standing position or while lying on the floor.

133. Have children carry a small ball while moving the arms and legs to add another element to increase each child's skills.

134. Doing exercises that stretch the body not only gives the large muscles exercise, but helps the body develop greater coordination and more flexibility. Holding any one position momentarily can increase the body's endurance and strengthen the muscles used for each of the positions. Simple yoga stretches would be appropriate for most children.

135. Children who have delays in large motor development should be encouraged to participate in the activities at whatever level they are comfortable. Activities can be adapted to accommodate their lower skill level. Minimally, nearly all children can participate at the level of being an observer. Parallel activities using the same muscle groups, but at a less demanding level, may also be provided for these children.

136. Wheelchair participants should be encouraged to observe and participate at the level they can be successful. Some of these children may need to have adaptations made or special large motor activities designed for them by an adaptive physical education teacher or occupational therapist.

STRATEGIES FOR SMALL MOTOR DEVELOPMENT

137. There are an unlimited number of hand activities that can be used with young children to promote and support their small motor development. These can be made available through interest centers in the classroom where the children can work on them independently as well as through planned activities involving group participation. Having a variety of materials available for children to use during choice times also helps promote children's engagement in small motor activities. Some examples of activities for the development of eye-hand coordination include the following:

  o Stringing beads, macaroni, or circular cereal pieces
  o Using LEGOS and other small building materials
  o Practicing lacing shoes
  o Making vertical, horizontal, and diagonal folds with paper
  o Using pegboards, such as Light-brite, to create patterns
  o Screwing and unscrewing nuts and bolts
  o Practicing buttoning and unbuttoning
  o Practicing manipulating snaps and zippers
  o Using sewing cards to make a variety of designs
  o Tearing paper in different shapes to make a collage
  o Using finger paints to create designs on paper

138. Clay (or play dough) is a good medium for children to manipulate. For a beginning activity, children can roll the clay into long rolls to make clay pots or bowls by putting the long rolls in a circle and then stacking them on each other. Or they can make individual letters and numbers from the clay rolls. Encourage the children to make other objects by rolling the clay into balls and creating other free-form figures.

139. Have children make telescopes by rolling up sheets of newspaper or colored construction paper, taping them in place, and then decorating them.

140. If a child has difficulty cutting with scissors, try a progression that begins with cutting a fringe on a piece of paper, cutting off the corners of a piece of paper, cutting simple shapes out of paper that have been outlined with heavy dark lines, or cutting out pictures in magazines that have been outlined with heavy black lines.

141. Have children tear different shapes or figures from newspapers or magazines and then create designs with these by pasting them on a piece of plain construction paper.

142. Have finger puppets available for children to use for creating dialogues or stories independently. Later encourage them to interact with other children to create group stories. This is an excellent way to practice finger movements to increase finger dexterity.

143. Sorting various shaped objects into similarly shaped containers helps children develop the small muscles of their hands. Have them do this sorting both visually and by touch (closing their eyes and feeling the shapes).

144. Have children practice paper weaving to make various designs. As they progress, they can create placemats for use in your setting or at their home.

145. The ability to use crayons and pencils will vary with chronological age and the small motor development level of the child. As a general practice, work from large crayons and pencils to smaller sized crayons and pencils. Washable markers as well as larger round watercolor brushes work well for children.

146. If tracing around shapes and objects with a crayon is too difficult for a child, have him trace geometric shapes and other forms with his fingers. This will help both his sense of form and his visual-motor coordination.

147. Have children trace and then color shapes that gradually increase in complexity of outline. The degree of control of finger movements required of the children becomes greater as the outlines become smaller and more complex. This activity can easily be adapted to a parallel activity for children who have difficulty with fine motor tasks.

148. With dull scissors, have children cut pieces of clay or play dough into designs or familiar objects.

149. Cutting activities of all kinds help strengthen the hands and fingers of children in addition to providing eye-hand coordination practice. If a child has difficulty cutting, have him start out by cutting out large circles and then decreasing the size. Progress to more difficult shapes and then on to pictures as the child is ready.

150. Painting with watercolors or tempera paints provides children with a fun way to develop and use their fine motor skills. Let them experiment with color, different shapes and forms, and pictures.

151. Use toothpicks to have children create different designs, objects, and figures (toothpicks make great stick people!). This is best done by having them glue toothpicks onto construction paper or lightweight cardboard.

152. Create sequences of finger movements. Demonstrate one sequence at a time and have the children repeat the sequence. Start out with a few finger movements in a sequence and gradually increase the number of movements per sequence as the children gain proficiency. Finger movements are good for finger dexterity, eye-hand coordination, and sequencing. Making shadow forms on a backlit wall adds the elements of mystery and interest to the exercise.

153. Mazes provide a fun way for children to develop their visual-motor abilities. Start with simple mazes, such as drawing a rabbit on the left side of a piece of paper, a carrot on the right side, and have the child draw a straight line connecting the two. You can create your own mazes to fit the range of visual-motor abilities within your group of children. See Form 7 in Appendix A for more examples of mazes.

154. Have children create mazes for other children to use. Run off copies of these mazes and have them available for the children to use during choice times.

155. Take the children out for a walk to collect one or two stones to bring back with them. Then have them paint an object, person, animal, or design on their stone.

156. Have the children collect small dry twigs from the ground of a nearby park. When you get back, encourage children to glue the twigs onto construction paper or lightweight cardboard to create designs and pictures. In a similar fashion, have them collect leaves and do the same project. As a variation, you can also have the children use both twigs and leaves for their pictures.

The above small motor activities help children develop eye-hand coordination skills that will later be applied to the writing process. An extension of these activities using crayons, pencil, and paper will be covered in Chapter 8.

6

Emotional and Social Development

Emotions impact all aspects of our daily lives—how we feel physically, how we feel about ourselves, how we interact with others, and how we engage in the learning process. Understanding of self and one's emotions along with one's ability to understand and be in social relationships are vital components in the education of children.

Strategies to help children develop emotionally and socially should be integrated and incorporated throughout children's learning time. Supporting their emotional and social development is a direct link to success as a learner. Emotional development is listed before social development to reflect the concept that development starts from within and proceeds in an outward or external direction.

Play is an important medium for younger children to develop their emotional and social development. It is as important to a young child as one's career is to an adult. Play teaches the child what the world is like in miniature form and consists of valuable learning experiences. It teaches children about themselves in relation to what they can and cannot do and how they relate to people, objects, situations, and events. It is through play that the child practices the tasks of life. To accomplish this, the child needs the help and support of nurturing and caring parents, child care providers, and teachers. The strategies included in this chapter focus on children's emotional and social development. The time commitment to the development of the emotional and social abilities of children should be in balance with the time commitment to their cognitive development.

Children with developmental delays and other special needs especially require a balanced focus on their emotional and social development to support them and give them the confidence to use their talents in ways that will enhance their learning without their getting discouraged or frustrated by their challenges.

STRATEGIES FOR SUPPORTING EMOTIONAL DEVELOPMENT

157. For children to grow emotionally, they need environments that make them feel physically safe. This is accomplished by paying attention both to the physical facility relative to the safety of the children and to how they are treated by both adults and children in their environment.

158. Children feel emotionally safer in environments in which they know what to expect. Adults working in all settings need to have clearly thought out expectations that are communicated to the children in attendance in ways they can understand. This is particularly important for emotionally insecure children. Predictability is also an important component for providing an emotionally and psychologically safe environment.

159. Consistency in expectations and structure for children in a child care or school program helps children feel a sense of psychological and emotional security. This has to do with schedules for the day, changes in staff, and follow-through on commitments made to children. It is important for children to know in advance when changes are planned.

160. Pair up an emotionally insecure child with a child who is secure and feels confident about himself. This is especially important during less structured times, when introducing a new activity, and when leaving the building for an adventure.

161. Child care providers and teachers should be aware of children's need to touch base with them frequently. It is best to preplan for this connection by providing children with appropriate ways and ample opportunities to do this. For shy children, adults will have to be the initiators of action rather than waiting for children to seek out a connection to touch base.

162. Giving genuine praise and positive affirmations to children while they are working on or completing a task gives less secure children the assurance that everything is okay. Praise often gives children the needed encouragement to persist in what they are doing and feel emotionally secure while doing it.

163. Feelings are very much a part of the inner world of children, who show these feelings by their behavior, facial expressions, and body language. Adults who work with young children can practice "reading feelings" by commenting to children about what they see and then observing their behavioral and verbal responses.

164. Acknowledge children's feelings whenever they use feeling-related words. Encourage them to describe what the feeling feels like inside of them. They may first connect with these feelings through the parts of their body such as having a stomach or head that hurts. Teach appropriate feeling words to the children you are working with through the use of pictures, actions, and events that simulate the common experiences they encounter every day. Feeling words that young children can relate to include *happy*, *sad*, *angry* (*mad*), *scared*, *excited*, *loved*, and *worried*.

165. When children become more familiar with feeling words and can identify those mentioned above, expand their list to include feelings like *fear*, *joy*, *peace*, *surprise*, *jealousy*, *caring*, *nervousness*, and others as they come up during conversations and activities. Find magazines that have good pictures of people who are doing activities or interacting with other people to whom children can relate. Have children look through these pictures and find people expressing each of the listed feelings.

166. Use pictures to connect feeling words to their meanings when teaching these words to children. These can vary from simple facial expressions to complex actions that convey feelings through body language. Magazines and children's books are rich sources of pictures for children to explore for examples of different feelings.

167. Reading children stories where feelings are expressed helps them understand that all people have feelings, what the feelings are, and how those feelings are expressed. See Form 9 in Appendix A for an activity about sharing and talking about feelings.

168. Once children are able to attach labels to their feelings, it is important to work on how to handle their feelings. If a feeling is positive, children may simply need to share it with someone; if it is a negative feeling, help them to discharge the feeling in an acceptable way, such as writing a word or drawing a face to describe the feeling on a piece of paper, crumpling it up, and throwing it away. Minimally, one should help change a negative feeling to a neutral one.

169. Have children name all of the animals they know. Make a list of these with one or more identifying features for each. Have the children think about what each animal is like and then identify the one that reminds them (has some of the same qualities) of themselves. Children can then draw the animal and share with a small group of children why they chose the animal they did. This exercise helps children think about who they are and what qualities they have. See Form 8 in Appendix A for an example of an activity to do with children.

170. Encourage children to share their dreams with you and with each other. Dreams are one way in which children act out their feelings. To share dreams is a way children can get in touch with their feelings to understand better what is currently happening in their lives.

171. Carefully selected toys can be a medium through which children can engage their feelings and act them out. This can be done with an adult or other children. Puppets and other symbols of people, props that simulate experiences in children's lives, and stuffed animals are appropriate for this purpose.

172. Create quiet spaces and play spaces in your setting where children can choose to go when they want to engage in solitary play or just be by themselves.

173. Begin the process of teaching empathy to young children by first having them relate to animals. For example, show them a picture of a bird and have the children imagine what it is like to be a bird. You can help children bridge the gap between themselves and take the perspective of others by repeating this process using any number of different animals. See Form 11 in Appendix A for an activity to do with children.

174. Have a live animal in your setting whenever possible. Animals can provide bonding for all children, but more so for the child who is shy and unsure of himself in relating to other children and adults.

175. Access tools for relaxation such as listening to calming music, brain gym movements, yoga, and so forth (see Appendix B, Resources) when children need to slow down and become more centered. The Institute of HeartMath offers tools such as *Freeze Frame* to help children reduce stress and become more calm and focused.

176. Help children learn more about their feelings through dramatic play. See Form 10 in Appendix A for directions.

STRATEGIES FOR SUPPORTING SOCIAL DEVELOPMENT

177. Promote social development in all children through the use of experiences, materials, and interactions with others. The situations will vary, depending upon the stage of social development of the child. This means providing for children who have not yet reached the age of symbolic play as well as for those who have moved into realistic and cooperative play.

178. Play is a natural, spontaneous activity for most children. Children with developmental delays in the area of social development will need to be encouraged by child care providers and teachers to initiate interaction and participation with others. Pairing less socialized children with children who have good social skills is an effective way to start the socialization process for these children.

179. Symbolic play can initially be promoted by child care providers and teachers by interacting with children in the following ways:

- When the child engages in play spontaneously, comment on what he is doing. Reinforce the child's play by making a positive comment about what he is doing.
- Imitate the child's action by engaging in parallel play with the child.
- Make suggestions as to how the child may extend whatever he is doing by trying additional activities.
- Make suggestions to the child as to what he or the two of you can do with toys and other materials.
- Model symbolic play by initiating and showing the child what he can do with the play materials.

180. Toys are a viable, nonintrusive way of promoting social interaction between children with and without special needs. It is therefore imperative to have available a wide variety of toys that will interest children and will allow for children with physical limitations or other special needs.

181. Capitalize on children's natural interest in nature and animals to teach them some of the basic ideas about social behavior. This can be done by going out into nature and by observing how the various insects, birds, butterflies, and so forth interact with one another. Watching a formation of Canadian geese or other birds or animals that flock together can be especially informative for children when followed up by questions and discussions. When doing this, encourage children to share their insights based on their creativity and imagination.

182. Use nonfiction and fiction stories about animals, insects, and birds for learning about the social habits of these creatures in nature and about how we can use some of those behaviors to develop social skills among ourselves.

183. Activities that require taking turns and sharing should be integrated throughout the child's day in all settings. For some children, these skills will need to be taught directly through modeling by other children and through talking them through the steps involved.

184. Dramatic play is an effective way to help children learn to feel and take the perspective of another child. By role-playing various parts, children experience what it is like to be someone else. The roles they play may be very different from who they actually are. Discussions should take place at the child's level of understanding to help them express what it was like to be someone other than themselves.

185. Take your dramatic play outside and use props provided by nature, adding them as needed to create various scenes, events, and stories.

186. Help children recognize and respond to the feelings of others by continually modeling these behaviors whenever you can. To ensure that this takes place on a consistent basis, adults should have both planned times and spontaneous times when these behaviors are modeled.

187. Observe individual children to determine the types of interactions they use when playing or doing projects with other children. Watch for verbal/ conversational interactions, motor/gestural interactions (such as waving, pointing, and taking turns), or a combination of these. If a child is using one type at the exclusion of the others, or at a severely imbalanced level, make note of this. Plan how you can provide opportunities for this child to learn to use all of these interactions in more balanced ways.

188. Arrange social integration experiences requiring the least amount of adult direction and participation. This facilitates child-to-child interaction, as the shy child or less socialized child may tend to "shut down" when an adult comes onto the scene.

189. Teach problem-solving skills to children so that they can interact with each other independently of adults when it is appropriate. Problems that typically arise among young children include the taking of turns, sharing, cooperating for the good of the group, and resolving conflict in appropriate ways. Learning how to handle problems within the child's age expectation is important to their overall social development. See Form 13 in Appendix A for a step-by-step process to use in teaching problem solving.

190. "What to do if . . ." kinds of situations help children learn that they have choices about how to respond in social situations, given certain conditions and behaviors by other children. Children can share their ideas in "what if" situations directly or through role-playing various scenarios commonly found in social interactions. It is also important to practice the behaviors in simulated situations so that they can be more easily applied when actual situations are encountered.

191. Create a special place, such as a "peace table," where two children can go to settle their conflicts through the use of words rather than aggressive actions such as hitting. To do this successfully, children need to practice specific steps they can take to settle their conflicts whenever possible; these steps should be posted on the wall or table using pictures rather than words to convey the process for each step. Once children learn the process, they can be directed to go to the peace table when conflict arises. Eventually, most children will choose this way of settling conflicts independently. See Form 12 in Appendix A for guidelines and an example.

192. Teach children assertiveness skills so that they will not be victims of other children's bullying, either in a physical form or through the use of words. To do this, children may need adults to intervene when they see interactions heading toward trouble by stopping the behaviors and suggesting ways for children to compromise or to express their feelings in more appropriate ways.

193. After a conflict between children, ask those involved to replay what happened. Then help the children discover alternative ways of handling this situation by having them play out the situation in a more productive way.

194. Children form their opinions of their personal worth in a social context through their experiences and from the attitudes and behaviors directed toward them by others. To promote positive feelings of self-worth, child care providers and teachers need to create a variety of experiences and activities that allow different talents to emerge. Modeling a positive, constructive attitude toward all children encourages the children to do the same.

195. To help children share their interests and talents, set aside a time for children to have a talent show. This can be a time for children to demonstrate their talents and experience the talents of other children.

196. Give as much positive feedback to children as is warranted. When constructive criticism is needed by a child, give it privately, with a clear message that it is the behavior that is unacceptable, not the child.

197. Develop communication with the children to the extent that they are comfortable asking you or another child for help when it is appropriate. In giving help, use the attitude that you will show the child how to do something and support him while he is learning it.

198. *Self-talk* is internally directed, quiet verbalization of words. Teach children positive self-talk strategies that they can use while playing and working by themselves or with others to reinforce the message "I can do it."

199. Help children achieve positive self-esteem by modeling unconditional love and acceptance to them and by focusing on what is being learned or is done correctly rather than on what is not learned or is done incorrectly. As children observe and experience you doing this for them, they will begin doing it for other children.

200. Teach children to tune in to what makes them feel peaceful or calm and what makes them feel restless or jumpy. You can do this by playing different kinds of music and asking how they feel when each type is being played. Continue the discussion with the children by having them share which objects, activities, and people help them feel calm or peaceful. Encourage them to "mentally connect" with these calming objects and activities or listen to or move gently to calming music whenever they are feeling restless and jumpy as a way they can calm themselves.

201. Make a "peace center" somewhere in your setting where individual children can go when they feel upset, need to slow down, or just need to be by themselves for a brief time. In the space, have calming music available with headphones and soothing objects, such as stuffed animals, for the children to hold while they are there. Encourage children to choose someone in their setting to go with them to share the experience when it is appropriate.

202. As children are ready to understand intentions behind behavior, introduce this concept to them. Some actions can be labeled "helpful and appropriate" or "inappropriate" based on the intention of the act. For example, when a child touches another child, it can be with the intent of calling the child's attention to something positive, or it can be with the intent of annoying the child.

203. As children become more discerning, they will learn to react differently to the actions of other children when they are able to differentiate the intention behind the action. With young children, it is a good practice to start out by giving the individual the benefit of the doubt. This means that one makes the assumption that the intention behind the behavior was meant to be helpful, not hurtful.

204. When planning cooperative activities, games, and projects for young children, always build in opportunities for young children to become more socially aware and to develop their social skills. It is also important to respond spontaneously to "teachable moments" for increasing children's knowledge as social beings.

205. Access such resource books as *Creating Balance in Children: Activities to Optimize Learning and Behavior,* which is listed in the References and Recommended Reading section of this book.

Given sensitivity, knowledge, and experience, teachers and child care providers can adapt most experiences and activities to meet the individual needs of children, regardless of where the children are in their emotional and social continuum of development.

Basic for all children, however, is the need to belong. According to Abraham Maslow, belonging is an essential and prerequisite human need that has to be met before one can achieve a sense of self-worth. Since a sense of belonging can best be supported in a social context, it is important that all child care, early childhood, and school settings have a strong emotional and social component to develop and support this area in all children.

7

Guiding and Modifying Children's Behavior

Behavior is a complex phenomenon that child care providers and teachers work with every day as they interact with young children. Guiding and modifying this behavior is a large part of their job.

Focusing on an approach emphasizing *guidance* rather than *punishment* for dealing with behavior helps children learn positive alternative ways of correcting inappropriate behavior. It also teaches them to solve problems in socially acceptable ways. The punishment approach to managing behavioral problems may stop the inappropriate behavior, but it does not lead to learning socially acceptable ways of behavior or the developing of positive self-esteem.

GENERAL STRATEGIES FOR GUIDING CHILDREN'S BEHAVIOR

206. Respond to the child's behavior as a form of communication. Ask yourself, "What information or feelings is the child trying to communicate to me?" Respond to the child to see if your understanding of what he is showing through his behavior actually results in the child changing his behavior. For example, if a child is feeling crowded and needs more space, he may act out or refuse to join in group activity. He may push himself into the group and cause problems for the other children. Acknowledging the child's need for space, you can prevent this problem by having him sit near the group without participating directly with it. Eventually, the child will learn to choose acceptable ways to handle his need for space independently, once he becomes familiar with his feelings and can identify them.

207. Think of a child's inappropriate behavior as **mistaken behavior** rather than misbehavior. The goal is to help the child learn from his mistake, not to punish him for making it.

208. Believe that negative behavior can be changed to positive behavior once the appropriate intervention or the best way to teach the child a new behavior is determined.

209. Separate the behavior from the child. It is the behavior that you cannot accept, not the child. It is important that adults differentiate the behavior from the child. This supports the child for who he is as a person and that it his behavior that is not appropriate for the situation.

210. As a first approach to dealing with young children's mistaken behavior, assume they have not been taught the appropriate behavior. Teach them by modeling the necessary behavior and helping them to understand what to do in a given situation.

211. If a child repeatedly engages in mistaken behavior, look for possible reasons for the inappropriate reactions to everyday experiences and interactions with others. Possible reasons include the following:

- A mismatch of the child with his curriculum, his working materials, or his experiences
- Difficulties in the child's life away from school
- Ignorance of the appropriate behavior needed for the situation
- Ill health due to inadequate nutrition or sleep or health problems
- The existence of a neurodevelopmental disorder

212. If stress or frustration is the primary reason for a child's poor behavior, consult with the child's parents to enlist their help in diffusing or eliminating the cause of the child's stress.

213. Observe the child behaving inappropriately to determine the degree of severity of the behavior and to see if there is any pattern present, such as certain times of the day, certain activities, and so on. Make note of this. If a pattern emerges, evaluate what is usually happening during the times this behavior occurs and use that as your starting point for creating interventions. Refer to Form 15 in Appendix A for an example that can be used for recording behaviors.

214. Make a clear statement to the child that a problem exists and then encourage the child to use words to help solve the problem. For example, the adult might say, "We have a problem. Please use whatever words you can to tell me about what you think the problem is so we can solve it."

215. If a child does not understand the words chosen to help him solve the problem, demonstrate the appropriate behavior through gestures and facial expressions. Then demonstrate alternative appropriate behaviors for the situation.

216. Teach children acceptable alternative behaviors through the use of pictures. This can be done by creating pairs of pictures showing appropriate and inappropriate behaviors for given situations. When children are familiar with these and understand their meaning, use the pictures to cue the child to use appropriate behavior when you see him initiating an inappropriate behavior.

217. Use toy people and puppets to demonstrate acceptable behaviors for common experiences and events. Let the children replicate what you show them and expand upon your ideas. They may then role-play the same situations using children playing different parts to demonstrate appropriate behaviors in various situations.

218. Avoid the use of negative labels in talking with children about their mistaken behavior. Due to young children's limited development and experience, they tend to internalize negative comments, begin to see themselves as negative, and then respond accordingly.

219. Change poor behavior by first correcting it through teaching alternative behavior. If this is not sufficient to correct the child's behavior, use techniques that will be considered by the child to be helpful rather than punitive.

220. If the behavior that occurs is a group problem rather than an individual problem, use the classroom format to identify and explore alternative ways to solve the problem.

221. Videotape the behavior of an individual child or of a group during different times of the day. Help the child or children identify examples of appropriate behaviors. Do not identify any individual child's mistaken behavior publicly.

222. If a child is engaged in a mild, nondistracting form of inappropriate behavior, ignore the behavior. Point out acceptable behaviors by calling the group's attention to examples of appropriate behaviors in the given situation or circumstance.

223. Encourage children to work toward a change in their inappropriate behaviors by improvement in small steps if a total, immediate change is not achievable. Also assure them that, with continued practice, they will be able to reach the desired behavior in the future.

STRATEGIES FOR MODIFYING CHILDREN'S BEHAVIOR

224. For children who do not respond readily to teaching-type interventions to change their behaviors, a more extensive approach, often referred to as a **behavior management plan**, is needed. The goal of this plan is to weaken and eventually correct mistaken behaviors over a period of time. See Form 14 in Appendix A, Steps in Changing Behavior.

Use the following steps to create a behavior management plan for a child:

Step 1. Make a list of the child's unacceptable behaviors for which you wish to create a behavior management plan.

Step 2. Prioritize the behaviors from high need for change to those least needing change. For young children, it is best to work on one behavior at a time. Changing one behavior often results in the change of other behaviors.

Step 3. Decide on a goal for the specific behavior you want to change and the appropriate alternative behavior to replace it.

Step 4. Assess where the child is relative to where you would like him to be. Do this by establishing a baseline of the frequency of occurrence of this behavior by observing and recording how often the behavior takes place over a three-day period. You may wish to restrict the recording of behavior to a specific time period during the day. See Form 15 for an example on how to record these behaviors.

Step 5. Decide on the intervention to use to help the child change his behavior.

Step 6. Every time the behavior occurs, immediately apply the intervention. Be consistent in using this intervention each time the behavior occurs.

Step 7. Record every time the targeted behavior occurs. Do this on the same chart you used to establish the child's baseline of frequency for this behavior. Your intervention is successful if the behavior is decreasing in frequency. Keep in mind that habituated behavior often changes in small steps.

Step 8. Evaluate the effectiveness of the intervention. If there is little or no change in the frequency of the child's targeted mistaken behavior, try a different intervention.

225. When you are using a behavior management plan to change a child's inappropriate behavior to a positive behavior, use reinforcers such as social reinforcers (smile, touch, etc.), a choice of activity options, or rewards that are age appropriate and meaningful to the child whose behavior you are trying to change.

226. Use **time out** (where the child is sent to a designated place by himself) as a last resort. If you need to use this approach, all adults in the child's setting need to be consistent as to which behavior for a specific child warrants a time out period. The place used for a time out should be very dull to the child. Any time out for a young child should consist of no more than one to five minutes (the purpose of the time out for a young child is to stop a behavior or to redirect the behavior to a more appropriate form).

227. For a child who needs time out as an intervention, teach him ahead of time that the purpose of the time out is to allow him to gain control of his behavior. Use time out as a supportive learning tool rather than as a punishment.

228. When a time out is needed for a child, follow these steps:

Step 1. Briefly tell the child why he is getting time out; that is, he hit Joey.

Step 2. Do not lecture or demean the child.

Step 3. Calmly escort the child to the designated time out location.

Step 4. Set a timer for the number of minutes the child is to be in time out.

Step 5. When the child's time is up, simply direct the child to rejoin the other children.

229. If you need to take action to stop a behavior, use signal interference. Let the child know he is doing something unacceptable by a raised eyebrow, a frown, or a shake of your head. Define limits succinctly and reasonably, with consequences clearly understood. If improper behavior occurs, activate the consequences immediately following the behavior. Be consistent in doing this whenever the behavior occurs.

230. If you have tried several approaches with little or no success in changing a child's erroneous behavior to socially acceptable behavior, inform the child's parents and cooperatively seek out other resources to help the child.

STRATEGIES FOR CHILDREN WITH ATTENTION PROBLEMS

231. Attention problems exist in several forms: not being able to focus attention on a purpose or task, inability to sustain attention for a period of time, and impulsiveness or **distractibility**. However, it is important to keep in mind that many young children display some of these behaviors as a function of their age and their response to informal and formal structure in the preschool setting or school setting. For these children, it is important to teach ways to adapt to the environmental demands.

232. For the children who demonstrate an excess of these behaviors, more extensive interventions are needed to help them increase their focusing and attending behaviors. Interventions such as specifically designed behavior management plans and consultation with a nutrition expert regarding diet can often help these children improve their engagement in the learning environment.

233. Certain colors have been found to have a positive effect in helping children feel calmer and to help keep their attention longer. To use this intervention, have several colors available in your setting. Different colored construction paper and carpet squares are easy to obtain and use. Have an assortment of these available so that children can select the color that makes them feel calmer and more comfortable (generally blues and greens). They can use their color to sit on, place beside them while they are working on a project, or use as a placemat. Since young children are very changeable, they need to be able to select the color that makes them feel good on a daily basis or more often if needed.

234. Always obtain a child's initial attention through eye contact.

235. For children who are easily distracted, plan for their seating and work area to be away from the potential distractions caused by being close to a window, near a main traffic pattern of the room, and near other distracting children.

236. Reduce the amount of external stimuli in your setting whenever appropriate. Hanging mobiles and having an excessive number of pictures and objects around activity areas add to the distraction factor for children who have difficulty paying attention and staying on task.

237. Children who have attention difficulties need consistent routines and more structure than other children. The degree to which they need these is dependent upon their inattentiveness relative to their age expectation.

238. Play music that is relaxing during transition times to help calm children and move them into a new task or project more comfortably. Music can make children less vulnerable to distractions.

239. Children who have attention and distraction problems do better when working in smaller groups rather than larger groups. Whenever possible, use a small group approach for activities with these children. Ideally, start with groups of three and gradually increase the group size as children are better able to focus and sustain attention.

240. Give one-step or two-step directions. Check for understanding of each step. When possible, pair visual demonstrations with verbal input.

241. Give the active child only one task to do at a time.

242. Use a timer to assist the child in remaining focused. Set the timer to coincide with the amount of time you perceive the child is able to sustain attention. Start with short periods of time and gradually increase the time as the child increases his ability to concentrate.

243. Allow the active child many opportunities for physical movement throughout the day. Individual and group play times help achieve this goal for the child.

244. If you sense the activity level of the group of children is increasing, stop whatever the children are doing. Have the children relax in place for one minute. A rag doll posture or other relaxing postures along with deep breathing (from the stomach) have a calming effect on children. These procedures may need to be used more often for the higher energy children in your setting. The eventual goal is for children to sense when they need to stop and relax, initiating this activity for themselves.

245. Young children naturally talk to themselves while engaging in play and other activities. Encourage children to use this self-talk technique to help themselves stay calmer and more attentive to what they are doing.

246. Pair active children with calm children for parts of the day that require the most concentration. Do this also when assigning children to groups. Balance the types of children you place in each group.

247. Allow the active child to have only the necessary materials for his current activity or project at his work space. Also allow the child to either stand or sit while working. Often an active child prefers to stand and be able to be more mobile.

248. Have a variety of stuffed animals available for children to hold during listening times. Cue them to listening by telling them their responsibility is to teach the animal to listen by how they listen.

249. Children should receive frequent accolades for their efforts to listen, pay attention, and stay with an activity for appropriate periods of time. This can be done through the use of words, gestures, and facial expressions. If a child does not respond to these social rewards, you may need to consider a "token" system. Here a child can earn tokens for special privileges in your setting or in the home setting. Rewarding the child when he is engaged in appropriate behaviors gives him the message that he can be successful. It also reinforces repetition of the behaviors you expect from the child. Although this may be helpful initially, extensive use of material rewards is not recommended as it often promotes the need for an external control system rather than developing an internal control system.

250. When the child with attentive, impulsive, or distractive behaviors is engaging in inappropriate behavior, tell him what he should be doing instead of what he should not be doing. This helps the child understand what is expected of him and avoids setting the child up to engage in another inappropriate behavior.

251. A child who has attention problems should be given ample opportunity for success to teach him he can control his behavior.

252. Keep a positive attitude toward children with attention difficulties. Acceptance, encouragement, and acknowledgement of their strengths are important for them to have a positive attitude about themselves. This serves as a foundation for all social relationships and all learning behaviors.

253. Talk with the parents of a child who has chronic inattention problems. Too much sugar in a child's diet, lack of sleep, and other environmental conditions may be contributing factors. Correcting these can result in increased attention in the school setting.

STRATEGIES FOR AGGRESSIVE AND WITHDRAWN BEHAVIORS

Aggressive Behaviors

254. Hitting, noncompliance (where a child does not comply with an adult's request), and teasing are behaviors exhibited at times by most young children. The child who is considered aggressive demonstrates one or more of these behaviors more frequently and more intensively. In working with this type of child, identify the aggressive behaviors, the frequency and severity of the behaviors, and in what context the behaviors take place.

255. As a first step, view aggressive behavior as learned behavior. As such, it can be modified and changed through a learning process, given the correct interventions. The adult's responsibility is to find what works for a particular child.

256. Develop a word list of what you consider to be aggressive behaviors. Find pictures that illustrate each of the behaviors you have identified and match these with the word list. Share this list with the children and talk about why these behaviors are not acceptable in your setting. Post this list in an appropriate place as a reminder for the children who need it.

257. When a child persists in engaging in aggressive behaviors, consult with the child's parents to determine whether these behaviors also occur in the home and neighborhood settings. If so, work cooperatively with the parents to find effective and consistent ways to intervene with the intent of decreasing aggressive behaviors in all settings. If the child does not display these behaviors in any other setting, evaluate what is happening in your setting to put these behaviors into motion.

258. Use a behavior management plan, such as the one mentioned previously, to decrease and eventually eliminate aggressive behaviors. Time out is also an effective intervention for children with aggressive behaviors. In all cases, be clear about the consequences of the behaviors and be consistent in using them.

259. Intervene early. If you see a potentially explosive situation, get to the child quickly to help him regain control. Use your presence, where you physically go to the child and either stand or sit by him rather than talk to him from across the room.

260. When you stop to redirect a child's aggressive behavior, do so calmly and in a matter-of-fact way. Help the child regain control by your calm, controlled manner.

261. In group discussion, talk about ways children can express their feelings in nonviolent, nonaggressive ways, such as using words instead of actions, talking to a friend, talking to a pet, or sharing their feelings with an adult whom they trust.

262. Give children true-to-life, concrete examples when discussing these issues. For example, you might suggest, "Suppose Ann poked you. What would you do? What are all the things you could do that are nonviolent to let Ann or an adult know how you felt about being poked?"

Withdrawn Behaviors

The withdrawn child generally spends as little time as possible with other children or adults, especially when he is in settings away from his home. When in the presence of others, this child either engages in independent, parallel play or simply observes the others without participating.

Group situations compound the difficulty for the withdrawn child. When someone talks to him, he is unlikely to respond, or if he does, he will limit his answer to one or two words. It is difficult for this child to make eye contact or smile at another adult or child other than his family. This behavior becomes even more extreme in the presence of others. For this type of child, toys, books, and other inanimate objects are more comforting and less threatening than people.

263. If you have a withdrawn child in your setting, it is important to talk with the child's parents to determine how their child relates to others in the home and neighborhood settings. If possible, find the cause for the withdrawn behaviors. Check if the child has been shy or withdrawn from birth or if this is a more recent occurrence, that is, at the onset of attending preschool, after some trauma, and so on. The reason for these behaviors could also be due to lack of exposure to social situations, the pressure of cultural expectations, the personality of the child, or how the child was treated when he initially tried to communicate or interact.

264. Sometimes withdrawal is a way for a child to avoid a painful situation based on the child's previous experience with people. Determining the cause can help the adults working with the child to create ways of encouraging him to begin to participate in social and task situations.

265. Encourage the shy or withdrawn child to participate initially at the level of communication that is most comfortable for him. This may involve the sharing of pictures with no verbal interaction. If the child attempts communication at this time, pay close attention to him and encourage his participation.

266. Accept where the child is and proceed from that point in helping him interact to a greater degree with his environment.

267. Encourage the withdrawn child to communicate through puppets of characters or animals. This takes the focus off the child himself.

268. Children who are withdrawn can often relate to pet animals. Have a fish, rabbit, or guinea pig in your setting if other children in that setting are not allergic to them. This can serve as a first step to begin relating to other children.

STRATEGIES FOR PROBLEM SOLVING

269. Teaching problem solving to young children at a level that is appropriate for their experience and age encourages them to respond to their world with a sense of competence and independence. Included in the problem-solving process is the ability to make choices and decisions. This too can be taught to young children. The first step in implementing this process is to be aware of the daily life experiences of children and the challenges that these experiences generate. This should be the context in which problem solving and decision making are taught.

270. Read stories to children about the kinds of situations similar age children encounter in their everyday lives. Introduce various types of situations to the children and discuss with them how most children respond to these situations and successfully work them out. Children can then share some of their own experiences and explain how they were resolved.

271. Create a series of situations, either verbally or through pictures, where children are engaged in experiences that require problem solving. Have children role-play the various situations, generating as many solutions to a problem as they can. Have each child share which solution feels best to them, helping them put their feelings into words.

272. Use games to provide children with practice in decision making and problem solving.

273. For the child who has difficulty making decisions, narrow his choice to two options, and then have him choose the one he prefers. Gradually increase the child's options until he becomes comfortable with making decisions. Eventually his decision-making skills will improve, as will his confidence in himself.

274. Teach a simple problem-solving process to the children. The basic steps to this process include the following:

1. Recognizing that a problem exists
2. Using pictures (facial expressions) to show how having the problem makes him feel
3. Using words to share the problem with someone else
4. Thinking of ways to solve the problem
5. Choosing one thing to take action on
6. Trying it out to see if the problem gets solved

Refer to Form 13 in Appendix A for a more complete outline of these steps.

275. Provide a variety of opportunities and experiences for children to practice decision-making and problem-solving skills. Let the children who grasp the idea quickly help the children who have more difficulty with this process.

276. Support children in their efforts to make their own decisions and solve the problems they encounter, even when the results are not successful.

277. Encourage parents to promote decision making and problem solving in the home setting, reminding them to provide the necessary guidance for their child to be successful. For example, choices can be made about what clothes to wear and what to bring to school for a snack.

Children's behaviors are purposeful and meaningful to them and are an important way in which they communicate with others. Adults need to tune in to the behaviors of children, interpret what they mean, and then respond accordingly. When children's behaviors take the form of mistaken behaviors, it is the adult's responsibility to note the current behavioral level of the child and intervene to transform inappropriate behavior into socially acceptable behavior. The strategies listed in this chapter can form the basis for this process.

8

Preparatory Writing, Reading, and Math Skills

These skills are the foundation of future academic learning for all children. How these teachings are first presented to children influences the attitude they will develop toward learning. Teaching skills in advance of a child's developmental readiness or in inappropriate ways often results in frustration that could lead to a negative attitude toward future learning. Children with developmental and other disabilities are particularly vulnerable in this regard.

Current research about how writing and reading are learned, how children make sense of their world through playful exploration, and how the brain works all support the concept that writing and reading are outgrowths of the same need to communicate that children use to express themselves orally and pictorially. *Emergent literacy* is the term used currently to describe this process. As such, it is viewed as a natural developmental process that occurs in a sequence of stages for all children.

Environments rich in a variety of books and adults who model a love for writing and reading best promote a child's natural urge to engage in these activities.

The preparatory math strategies included in this chapter are related to the concept of quantity, size, time, and measurement.

The emphasis of the strategies in all of these areas is on creating experiences in which children can explore and experiment with preparatory writing, reading, and math skills in ways that are consistent with a developmental point of view. Since the natural development of writing and reading occurs simultaneously in children, these two areas will appear together. Before using these strategies, it is helpful to know as much as possible about each child. Areas to consider include the following:

- A child's strengths and limitations
- A child's pattern and progress in learning and development
- Any health-related issues that may affect learning
- Any major changes or transitions taking place in the child's life
- Any recent trauma that has occurred in the child's life
- The child's current level of functioning in preparatory writing, reading, and math skills

See Form 19 in Appendix A for a suggested format for gathering this data.

PREPARATORY WRITING AND READING STRATEGIES

278. A generally accepted sequence for the development of a child's writing proceeds from

- o pretending to write by scribbling horizontally, to
- o scribbling in which the features of real letters appear, to
- o the writing of real letters, to
- o writing words with invented spelling, to
- o writing words with actual spelling.

Observe the level at which each child in your setting is performing, record the date of your observation, and watch for movement to the next level. You may adapt Form 17 in Appendix A for this purpose.

Note: Some children with developmental delays may need to start at a level that comes before the above-listed sequence.

279. Set up a writing area for children with all the necessary implements, such as markers, crayons, pencils of varying sizes, unlined paper, lined paper with large spaces between the lines, tablets and pads of various sizes and colors, and colored chalk with small blackboards. Encourage children to experiment with the various materials you have provided when they have unstructured time. Let the participation be at the child's level of readiness.

280. Combine color or music or both with eye-hand activity whenever you can to expand the sensory stimulation of the experience. This increases the quality of the experience for the children and facilitates the integration of their motor activity.

281. Have a variety of colored paper and writing tools for children when they engage in scribbling or preparatory writing activities. Let them choose the combination of colors that feels the best to them.

282. Designate a place where children can go to listen to music with headsets while they are doing their scribbling and preparatory writing activities. Music that simulates the rhythm of the heartbeat (about 60–70 beats per minute) is excellent for this purpose. It sets a steady, comfortable pace that is already an intrinsic part of the child.

283. Drawing circles, semicircles, and straight lines in horizontal and vertical positions precedes combining these shapes into letters. Allow the children many opportunities to have fun making these forms using different colors and different media such as clay and sand trays (sand placed in trays) in addition to drawing them on paper.

Note: This activity can also be used as a parallel activity for children to use when other children have moved on to making actual letters.

284. Provide the opportunity for children to "feel" the letters by having them put the letters into movement. To do this, they can lie on the floor and curl around to make the shape of each letter. Have them start out by making the easiest letters, such as O, L, C, and so forth. For children who cannot create the shapes of the letters on the floor, use masking tape and form letters for them on a table. Have them trace out the shape of each letter with their hand, naming it as they do so.

285. Pair children of about the same height together and have them form letters through the movement of their bodies. Music enhances these movements and makes this activity more fun. When children become proficient at doing this, have one pair of children do a movement for the rest of the children. Have the second group then guess what letter has been formed.

286. Have children practice writing in the air with their dominant hand, first with their eyes open so they can see the letter, and then by closing their eyes and feeling its shape.

287. Pair children and have them practice imaginary writing on each other's backs. Have them take turns doing this. Make a game out of this activity by having the child whose back is being written on guess what letter it is.

288. Use toothpicks to give children the opportunity to experience the shape of letters. Have them experiment with all the letters such as A and H that can be constructed with straight sticks. Later add circles and semicircles so that they can experiment with making the letters requiring those shapes, such as O and C. Then progress with combining circles, semicircles, and toothpicks for completing the most complex letters, such as B and D.

289. Use a flashlight to write shapes and letters on the ceiling, chalkboard, or wall. Have the children track the light with their eyes and the pointing finger of their writing hand while they name the shape or letter.

290. Provide tactile writing experiences for children through group experiences and as an independent choice during unstructured time. Cut letters out of various grades of sandpaper that children can finger-trace with the pointing finger of their dominant hand. Use colored glue, glitter, pipe cleaners, seeds, and so forth to create textured models for the children to finger-trace. Encourage the children to do finger-tracing with their eyes open until they are familiar with the shape of the letter and then with their eyes closed, visualizing the shape of the letter in their head while finger-tracing the letter. It is also a good practice to have them name the letter as part of the preparatory reading process while doing the finger-tracing and visualizing of the shape of the letter. As children become more advanced, they can give the sounds of the letter.

291. Have children experiment with using a different color for each letter when writing words singly or in sentences using inventive spelling.

292. To aid in their understanding of *left* and *right*, first create a vertical list of words. Have them make the first letter of each word green, and the last letter red. Remind the children to start a word at green and stop at red.

293. Small trays filled with sand or rice provide a good alternative for a writing medium for children who have not yet developed the fine motor control necessary to manipulate a pencil.

294. Encourage children to make shapes and letters with watercolor paints and brushes, working either from an easel or while sitting at a table. Using watercolors also gives them an opportunity to experiment with color.

295. Give children the opportunity to practice their fine motor skills by providing tracing paper and objects, shapes, and letters for them to trace.

296. Use games to encourage children to experiment with the letters of the alphabet, by playing with magnetic letters, letter dice, and other forms of letters.

297. Create or purchase alphabet cards having a picture of an object on them. Let the children make up games such as finding the first letter of their name, matching letters, and so forth. This can be done independently by one child or done in small groups.

298. Provide the children with a choice of alphabet books that have interesting and meaningful objects to go with each letter or word. When children are ready, encourage them to make their own alphabet books.

299. Have available computer alphabet programs that are specially designed for young children to learn letter recognition in a simple, fun way, not as lessons. Programs that have animated graphics and music are especially appealing to young children.

300. Label different areas and objects in your setting with colorful signs. This helps connect the child with the idea that words have meaning. Encourage children to make their own signs for their work areas or for their room at home by setting aside a special table with materials and letter templates.

301. Have each child decorate a shoe box that can be used as his individual mailbox at school. Have him print his own name on the box. If the child cannot do this, have an adult either do it or provide him with a stencil for printing his name. To help children understand that print has meaning, leave brief notes in each child's mailbox on a weekly or biweekly basis. These can be translated by an older sibling or a parent at home, or by an adult in the school setting.

302. Create a series of cards that have pictures of an action on them, such as *stand*, *sit*, *smile*, or *frown*. Label each card with the action word that best describes it. Take a few minutes each day to have the children perform some of the actions by holding up one card at a time. As they perform the action, have them say the word or words that go with the action. This exercise helps children link words with actions.

303. Based on her research with preschool children, Judith A. Schickedanz (1999) proposed the following sequential stages of children's natural development in the area of reading:

- o Retells stories from books with increasing accuracy
- o Shows awareness that print in books tells a story
- o Attempts to match telling of story with print in book
- o Wants to know what particular print says

To determine where each child is in his knowledge of natural reading skills, observe the child's interaction with books and stories. This can be done when children engage in imaginary play that is based on the information found in a book, or when two or more children share a book.

304. Bring children and books together by having a large variety of books available for children to look at and share with each other. This collection of books should be composed of make-believe stories, stories about animals, nature stories, and stories about young children and their daily adventures and challenges, and should be filled with colorful pictures.

305. Encourage children to bring their favorite books from home to share with the other children. Set aside a specific time each week when children can do this.

306. Remember that children love the familiarity of repetition and benefit from listening to their favorite stories over and over. Soon they take on telling the story in their own words, practicing the natural sequence of preparatory reading skills that match the telling of a story with the actual print in the book.

307. Invite people from the community to come and read to the children in your setting. Prepare guidelines for the visitors to use when they read to your group of children. Unless the visitor has had experience working with young children, it is best to provide the person with a book to read.

308. For the children who are ready for more extensive experiences in writing, provide them with the materials and support to engage in mock letter writing, using inventive spelling to write one- to three-line stories. Then have them read their story to another child, to a small group, or to one of the adults in your setting.

309. Before you read a new story to children, draw them into the context and experience of the story by focusing on one or two pictures in the story through a series of questions. Lead-in questions can include the following:

- Who and what do you see in this picture?
- What is happening in the picture?
- What do you think will happen next?
- What colors do you see in the picture?
- How do you feel when you look at this picture?
- What parts of the picture remind you of other stories you have heard or something that has happened to you?

310. Provide a tape recorder and some blank audiotapes in a special place in your room for children to use when making up their own stories. Teach the children to operate the tape recorder so that they can use it when they have a story to tell. Have them tell their story into the tape recorder, then give you the tape to transcribe their story for them. Give them the printed copy of their story and have them read it to you. They may want to illustrate their story and put it in a booklet form, to be added to as they create additional stories. If children really get into this activity, you may ask a parent to volunteer once or twice a week to do this project with the children.

311. After a field trip or other event, have the children share their experience by writing a story about it. Do this as a group and combine as many of the children's ideas as you can into the story. Once the story has been printed in words by you or another adult, post the story on the wall so that the children can practice reading the story on their own. They will read it by memory and put their own thoughts into the story. This will help them connect with the meaning and purpose of print and reading. If you have other adults available in your setting, creating small groups of children to write their experiences in story form is more effective than doing this activity in a large group with young children.

312. Read rhymes to children often. Choose a variety with differing rhythms. Once the children become familiar with the rhythms, have them clap to the rhythms while you read. To extend this experience, provide the children with simple percussion-type instruments such as sticks, bells, dried gourds, or small drums to use while you are reading the various rhymes.

313. When children become familiar with rhymes and can repeat some from memory, have them make up their own rhymes. Working as pairs often facilitates this process for children. Invite children to share their rhymes with other children and with the whole group.

314. Encourage the children to combine singing and musical instruments with the words of their rhymes when they share them.

315. Combining singing games with simple folk dances translates words and music into actions for children. These help children expand their vocabularies and help make words a fun part of their lives.

316. Word games are appropriate to use with young children when they can match and identify simple words. Word blocks and word bingo are examples of the types of games that can be used. Word blocks consist of a series of small plastic or wooden blocks with simple words pasted on their sides. Children use the word blocks to make up simple sentences. In word bingo, typical bingo cards are used, but simple words are pasted over the numbers. The number cards also have matching words pasted on them so that when a word is drawn, the child looks for the word on his bingo card. The same rules are followed as for regular bingo with numbers. A completed bingo card should consist of simple sentences.

317. Provide a variety of props for children to use in dramatic play. Encourage them to make up their own plays and perform them for the other children.

318. Read a variety of poetry to children. Invite a local writer of children's poems to come to your setting and read his poetry to the children. Have the poet share what it feels like to write and to share his poetry with others. As a follow-up, have a poetry-writing session with the children where they write short poems. To help young children choose what they want to write about, have them think of their favorite animal, toy, or object, and then have them write a few sentences about it in a poetry format. For children who cannot write real letters, let them use scribbling or mock writing and then tell an adult what they wrote so the poem can be transcribed into words.

319. Young children love to learn and use new words. Take as many opportunities as possible throughout the school day to call attention to a new word that comes up from experience. Also, plan to introduce the children to at least one new word each day, giving them the word in picture form, in action form when possible, and in word form. When appropriate, connect feelings with the word. Give as many examples as possible of how the word can be used in their daily lives.

320. Encourage parents to call their children's attention to everyday signs that occur repeatedly in their various environments.

PREPARATORY MATH SKILLS

321. Numbers should be introduced to children in the context in which they occur, such as in a child's age, on signs children see while traveling to and from school, on clocks, on calendars, and in stores. Have the children tell you where they see numbers being used in their everyday experiences. Make a list of these and have the children add to them as they discover additional places. Discuss the different ways in which numbers are used and what kinds of information we get from them.

322. Increase children's awareness of numbers and their one-to-one correspondence with quantity by telling them the names of numbers. Start out with 0 and add additional numbers as the children are ready. Carefully and clearly define the quantity associated with each number. This is best done by introducing objects, showing them pictures of the objects, naming the number of objects, and then writing the numerical symbol that represents the number of objects.

323. Use coarse sandpaper to make the numbers 1 to 9. Have children take turns feeling the shape of each number. Let them share what the shape feels like and use words to describe the shape. For children who have difficulty writing, have them place a piece of paper over the letter and rub a crayon over the letter shape to make an impression of the letter on their paper. Then have them cut out the number and keep it for future use.

324. Have each child choose his favorite number and draw or write it on his favorite color of paper. Often a child will choose the number of his age, so have several copies of each number for the children to use as models.

325. Play a matching number game by having each child use his favorite number to find the other children in the room who have the same number. When they have found all the children who have matching numbers, have those with the same numbers sort the numbers by color.

326. Collect shells, beads, seeds, various shaped pasta, and buttons. Put them into boxes or bags. Use these collections to sort and classify objects.

327. Use egg cartons or muffin tins to give children the opportunity to experiment with sorting objects. If you paint a number on each section, these can also be used for children to practice counting out the number of objects as it corresponds to the number written on each section.

328. Plan activities to help children become familiar with the terms *same*, *different*, *more*, *less*, *small*, *big*, or *large*. These terms are the abstract distinctions of numerical values.

329. Create opportunities for children to use counting in as many ways as possible throughout the day. During snack time, they can count the number of napkins and cups needed for each table. They can count the number of children at each table or in each work space. They can count the number of different toys they use during free playtime.

330. Have children practice making numbers by having them use the same techniques they used to make letters, only substitute numbers for the letters. Be sure there are plenty of examples of correctly made numbers available for the children to look at as models for their numbers.

331. Choose appropriate computer games for the children that will help them gain a better understanding of counting and the one-to-one correspondence between numbers and quantity. A game approach is better for young children than a skill approach.

332. An abacus serves as a wonderful introduction to numbers, as it is physical in form, yet abstract in concept. It was used as the first calculator and still provides a functional means for working with numbers.

333. Sequence and order are important for children's understanding of math processes. To let children experience these two concepts, provide them with "connect the dot" games for creating objects and pictures.

334. Set up a treasure hunt within your room or on the playground. Use a sequence of numbers as clues for locating the treasure. Restrict the range of numbers to the ones that are familiar to most children. Children also enjoy setting up treasure hunts for each other.

335. Make a pictorial representation of the schedule the children will be following each day on a large calendar (weekly or monthly). Divide it into A.M. and P.M. Check off each activity on the schedule as it is completed. This helps children feel a sense of sequence and order as they progress through the day. Numbering each activity gives children further experience with the sequence and order of numbers.

336. Construct games using popsicle sticks, beads, buttons, and so on to help children experiment with making associations between a number and its quantity. Allow children to experiment creatively with these in the ways they use them and in making up games from them.

337. Use singing games and rhymes, such as "one, two, buckle my shoe," or "one little, two little, three little kittens," to help children experience numbers and their sequence in a variety of contexts.

338. Children can experience time (and distance) by finding the answers to questions through physical action. For example, will it take longer to walk or to run to that tree? To demonstrate the difference, have two children line up an equal distance from the tree. Have one child walk while the other child runs to the tree. As children observe the outcome, they will be able to answer the question. Repeat this same procedure using different end points, different directions, and different objects to let children experience time and distance from this perspective.

339. Give children measuring (spatial) experience by having a sand tray (or one filled with rice), measuring cups, and measuring spoons available for them to experiment with the various sizes and the quantities they hold. Create a series of pictorial cards comparing the different sizes. Have the children determine which holds the most sand or rice, which holds the largest and which holds the smallest amount, which is the biggest cup, which is the smallest spoon, and so forth.

Preparatory writing, preparatory reading, and preparatory math activities for young children should be based on their level of applicability. There are unlimited fun-filled activities from which to choose. The strategies and activities listed here are just a beginning to the many possibilities.

9

Assessing Young Children

Assessment is a process whereby we systematically gather information about children from a variety of sources. When assessing young children, we need to be cognizant of their developmental patterns so that the types of assessments we use give us the most accurate results. The standards set by the school system should not solely determine what testing young children undergo. Certain situations may require the gathering of information about a child that goes beyond what schools require. Assessments for children should include both standardized and informal measures of their functioning in a variety of areas to gain an understanding of the "whole child."

Accurate assessment requires not only expertise, but also sensitivity on the part of the adults who participate in this process. Hunches and a sense of knowingness (often referred to as intuition) also play an important part in the assessment process. The following pages will detail some of the issues that arise in the assessment of young children and will offer strategies that can be used to accomplish this task.

CHARACTERISTICS OF YOUNG CHILDREN THAT AFFECT ASSESSMENT

Young children can be unpredictable in their reactions and behaviors to people and situations in their environment. Their responses can shift on a moment-to-moment basis. This affects the accuracy and reliability of assessment data and raises the issue of the size of the sample of behavior needed to adequately reflect a child's behavior, the circumstances surrounding the testing situation, and the time period needed to represent a true picture of the whole child. To draw wrong conclusions or mislabel a child is not only detrimental to the child but may lead to the setting of inaccurate expectations and programming that impacts a child's future learning.

340. Young children are often unable to explain themselves well. They demonstrate what they know and how they feel through their behaviors, rather than through words. Adults, therefore, must infer a child's thoughts and feelings from the child's behaviors. At best, what we infer has a good possibility of being an underestimate of what the child knows and can do.

341. A short attention span is typical of young children. This means that adults need to be patient, work with the child in short segments of time, and gather their information over an extended number of days.

342. Language is understood and expressed by young children at a very literal and concrete level. In assessing children, the adult should use a minimum of words that are at the level of the child's understanding.

343. Young children respond more readily to people, objects, and situations within a natural context. Assessment should take place in and utilize the resources of the child's normal environment whenever possible to ensure the authenticity of the results of the assessment.

344. When a child feels threatened by a testing situation or any part of it, he has the tendency to withdraw, act out, or "freeze." These defensive behaviors compromise a child's ability to share what he knows, which in turn results in an inaccurate picture of the child. If this happens, the adults who assess the child need to make note of these behaviors and the fact that the results from this assessment may not be accurate.

DEVELOPMENTAL PATTERNS

Growth begins and proceeds from the inner world of the child and is then expressed in the external world. In assessing young children, we can only measure the external manifestations of their inner growth processes. Sometimes we can get a hint of an emerging skill if we pay close attention to the qualitative aspects of a child's responses. When assessing children, we need to remember we are getting but a small glimpse of what any one child can do; growth is always further along than we can observe or measure externally.

The cognitive growth rate is most rapid between birth and about six years of age. Therefore, to get an accurate picture of where a child is in any one area at a specific point in time, we need to assess the child more frequently. This also makes assessment information less reliable in predicting a younger child's future performance than it is for older children.

Physiological maturation affects a child's learning and performance abilities. With young children, it is difficult, in many cases, to distinguish whether a slower rate of mastering skills is due to a slower rate of physiological maturation or due to some organic anomaly. This makes prediction of future performance based on current performance more difficult, if not impossible, making any long-term predictions for a child's future learning unreliable.

The child's innate abilities and the external manifestations of learning and capacity to do things are directly related to the number and types of stimuli present in a young child's early environment. This can make it difficult to discern how much a child's performance in any one area has been affected by inadequate exposure versus a more organic delay in the child's development. Therefore, assessment conclusions for younger children, especially those of preschool age, should be viewed as more tentative in nature. The presence of educated and caring parents will often result in a child who is more precocious and better adjusted to his environment and to people in general. Others who appear to be slow starters may not have had the exposure to events or to people who could teach them and guide them in those early years. These children, given a similar school environment and a reasonable period of time, can often catch up to other students.

However, testing these children may erroneously classify and label the late starters. This is a situation we want to avoid at all costs as it will be at the expense of children who have not had access to a variety of early environmental experiences to the degree that many children do.

PURPOSES FOR ASSESSING YOUNG CHILDREN

345. Working with children on a daily basis provides child care workers and teachers with a wealth of information about a specific child. Documentation of what is known about a child by the adults working with him should take place prior to making an assessment of that child (see Form 19 in Appendix A as an example for recording this information). This will help determine if and what additional information about the child is needed, how this information should be collected, and who should do the testing before an assessment process is initiated.

346. At times, a child care provider or teacher may have questions as to the functional level of a child or the area in which a child needs extra instruction or accommodation. Assessing a child's performance in the area of question is appropriate for matching instruction, materials, and activities with the child's level of need, known as the zone of proximal development (see Chapter 1).

347. Some type of assessment is often needed to determine what progress children are making and at what rate they are making this progress. Assessment of the child's ability from a documented starting point will provide an accurate accounting of the child's progress. Dates, how the skill or learning is assessed, and the materials that are used in making the assessments are important for an accurate measurement of a child's progress.

348. In cases where it is determined that a child is not making adequate progress, an assessment is warranted for the purpose of screening the child for developmental delays or possible disabilities that may require special attention and, in some cases, special education services.

349. Assessment for placement purposes (to see if a child meets special needs eligibility) is required when there is evidence obtained from screening assessments, documented lack of progress, and observations by the adults working with the child and the child's parents that substantiates the need for this type of assessment. This would be considered to be a comprehensive assessment requiring the involvement and input of all adults working with the child, the child's parents, and professionals such as special education teachers, psychologists, social workers, and so forth.

350. Once intervention begins, assessments are needed periodically to evaluate the effectiveness of the interventions for a specific child. These can be at the learning or behavioral level for children with or without special needs. Based on this assessment, a determination can be made as to whether or not a child's program needs to be modified.

351. All children at the present time undergo periodic statewide assessment under the No Child Left Behind Act. The results of these assessments are generally used by school districts to chart the academic progress of the students as a whole in that school district.

ASSESSMENT TOOLS AND TECHNIQUES

352. The selection of the procedures, materials, and criteria to be used in assessing young children must be done carefully and take into consideration the following factors:

- o The area of development, skill, or behavior to be assessed
- o The procedures and instruments that will provide the most relevant information with the least intrusion on the child
- o The child's primary language
- o The cultural background of the child
- o The child's communication skills
- o Conditions present that might have an impact on the child's performance (such as low vision or a physical disability)
- o The person(s) doing the assessment
- o The location where the assessment takes place

OBSERVATION

353. Observation of the child in his natural setting while engaging in routine daily activities should be a part of every child's assessment. This gives the best overall picture of the functional level of the child in many areas. This process consists of an adult watching the child, recording the actions of the child, and making intuitive assumptions regarding how the child feels about what he is doing. It is important to observe the quality of what the child does as well as his actions. See Form 17 in Appendix A for an example of an approach for recording a child's behavior.

354. Observe children in a variety of situations. The following examples are some of the observations that should be made:

- o Behaviors during routines (snack time, getting ready to go outside, cleaning up from an activity, etc.)
- o How the child interacts with various materials
- o How the child interacts with other children during playtime and also doing more structured, hands-on activities
- o How the child interacts with other adults
- o The extent to which the child engages in solitary play and uses his options for independent activity
- o How the child uses his solitary time
- o Behavior of the child in a group setting when it is being teacher-directed
- o General levels of performance in various areas of development, both in terms of what the child can do and in comparison to similarly aged peers

355. Write down the behaviors and the child's associated feelings as they occur by using charts and checklists designed for the appropriate age and developmental level of the child you are observing. It is best to try several methods for recording behaviors to see which one works best.

356. Observe children doing the same thing on a repeated basis to allow for the unpredictability of young children's behavior from day to day.

357. When you feel you have observed a child enough to be able to describe the behaviors and feelings the child demonstrates, analyze the data to determine the strengths, limitations, and functional levels of the child.

358. Look for patterns of behavior and feelings in the observational data you have collected about the child. Document these and use this information in determining goals for the child and how best to meet them.

INTERVIEWS

359. An interview consists of a series of questions or open-ended statements ("Tell me about Joe") that are used in accessing information about children from their parents and other adults who know and work with them. For the less skilled interviewer, it is advisable to use a more structured approach that consists of a series of specific questions created for the purpose of obtaining information about a child. See Form 19 in Appendix A.

360. If you make up your own questions for the interview rather than using an appropriate commercial form, focus on using open-ended questions (requiring more than a "yes" or "no" answer) rather than closed questions (requiring only a "yes," "no," or single word answer). An example of an open-ended question is, "Tell me some of the things that Joey enjoys doing most when he is at home." An example of a closed question is, "Does Joey like to play alone?" Closed questions are appropriate for accessing some information such as, "How old was Joey when his sister was born?"

361. Summarize the information you receive from each of the adults you interview about the child. Look for commonalities and differences. Analyze the information from the interviews to determine if there are any consistent themes or patterns that have relevance to working with the child.

STANDARDIZED TESTS

Standardized tests are created for the purpose of comparing a child's abilities or development in the areas of cognitive (thinking), emotional, social, physical, and adaptive behaviors to other children of similar age. These tests may be either *norm-referenced*, where the child's scores are compared to the norm or average behavior of similar-age children (such as on intelligence and achievement tests), or *criterion-referenced*, which measure a child's skills relative to skills taught or skills needed to perform a specific task.

362. Standardized tests are most often required when screening young children for developmental delays or disabilities for diagnostic purposes, for placement purposes, and for measuring a child's progress relative to his peers. There are a number of these tests available. It is usually the person trained to give these types of tests or the child study team that makes the decision as to which tests to use. If you have any questions regarding the options, consult the person who is coordinating the testing process or the person who will be administering the tests to the child.

363. Standardized tests consist of a series of items that require a specific response or follow a set of criteria that can be objectively scored. The norms for these tests are based on how sample populations of children of varying ages and grade levels have performed across the United States. Scores from standardized tests, such as the Kaufman Assessment Battery for Children, are most often reported as standard scores or **percentile scores**. Many of the developmental tests for young children also use age equivalency scores to report testing results. However, age equivalency scores are the least reliable way to report test scores and often lead to a misinterpretation of a child's skills and abilities. For example, to tell a parent his five-year-old child is functioning at a three-year-old level in a particular area is devastating to the parent as well as being misleading.

364. When interpreting test scores, it is necessary to understand the meaning of the score used for reporting test results in order to draw accurate conclusions about the performance of a specific child. This makes your explanation to the parents more understandable and more accurate. When evaluations are given within the context of special education, it is in the best interests of everyone to have the professionals who gave the tests report the results and what they mean to the parents and other members of the individual educational plan (IEP) team.

365. Standard scores are the most reliable test scores to use in interpreting the meaning of tests and communicating test results. Statistically, it is the most accurate representation of how a child performed relative to other children of similar age. Defined, a standard score is a score that has been normalized on a group of children across age groups.

A common number used to denote the midpoint of the average range is 100, give or take a few points for error in testing (the younger the child, the more error there is in testing). Any standard score that lies between 85 (±) error points and 115 (±) error points is considered to be within the average range. This includes 68% of the general population of children. Standard scores that are above 115 are considered to be above average and those below 85 are considered below average. Scores within these ranges can vary from somewhat above or below average to significantly above or below average.

366. For purposes of placement in special education programs, the quantitative standard score is generally used. For purposes of sharing information with parents, the terminology of above average, average, or below average is often used to convey how their child has performed relative to other children of the same age.

For every standard score, there is an equivalent percentile score ranging from approximately 1% to approximately 99%. These scores tell you the percentage of children who obtained higher scores and the percentage who obtained lower scores than the child tested. For example, if a specific child obtained a percentile score of 55 on a cognitive ability test, this means he did as well or better than 55% of the children used in the norm group. Furthermore, it means 45% of the children in the norm group did better than he did.

Given the fact that any percentile score between 25% and 75% is considered to be within the average range, this child scored at about the middle of the average range, demonstrating average cognitive abilities as measured by the test used. Percentile scores are easier to understand for adults who are not familiar with testing, but not as accurate statistically as standard scores.

Figure 9.1 illustrates a comparison of standard and percentile scores as represented by a bell curve distribution.

Figure 9.1   A Typical Distribution of Standard and Percentile Scores

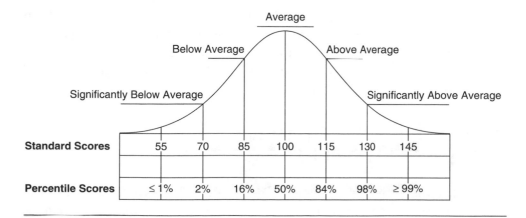

367. Age-equivalent scores are based on the performance of typical children at each age level. These scores are expressed as a numerical value by year and month of a child's age. Age-equivalent scores are easy to understand but are often misunderstood. If you use these scores for explaining test results to parents, use them with caution. In most cases, it is better to use either terminology denoting above average, average, or below average compared to similar age peers, standard scores, or percentile scores.

368. Use standardized tests and test scores only in conjunction with the other information you have documented about a child from samples of his work, daily performance in class, observation, and interviews. Remember, tests measure only a sample of behavior of a child for specific tasks in a given period of time. As such, they do not give the "whole picture" of a child. Information about how the child functions on a day-to-day basis at school and at home is necessary for getting an accurate picture of any child.

OTHER ASSESSMENT PROCEDURES

369. A planned approach to collecting and organizing samples of children's work is helpful in measuring a child's functional levels and progress. With this approach, samples of a child's performance on a variety of tasks over a set period of time (such as a month) are collected and filed. At the end of the month (or other time period such as fall and spring), these examples are shared and reviewed with the child's parents. For children who need a great deal of assistance, you may want to label which examples were done independently and which were done with assistance.

370. Keep one sample of a child's work from each week of attendance. You may prefer to choose a sample of the child's artwork, attempts at writing, or both. Be sure to date each sample, so that every few months you can look at these samples to evaluate the progress of the child in these areas. Include as many areas as you wish to track a child's progress. Sharing these with parents every three months is also an excellent way to keep them abreast of their child's performance and progress.

371. Creating simulated tasks that place children in a variety of situations can be beneficial in assessing children's functional abilities. This approach can be used whenever one is unable to observe and assess a child while he engages in these tasks in a natural setting or when a more detailed observation of the child is needed. For example, having a child sort objects and count them for you gives you an understanding of that child's knowledge about categorization and one-to-one correspondence.

ASSESSMENT OF CHILDREN WITH SPECIAL NEEDS

372. Children with developmental delays and other disabilities need special consideration in determining what assessment procedures and tests should be used in order to get an accurate picture of their functional skills in specific areas.

To determine the best assessment choices, consult with early childhood special educators and psychologists who are well-versed in testing young children.

373. Testing of children with special needs requires a team approach where professionals can convene to decide on the information needed regarding a specific child, the assessment tools to be used, where the testing will be performed, and who will do the testing. Parents and child care providers or teachers need to be members of this team.

374. Monitoring of a child with special needs (a form of assessment) should be an ongoing part of the child's program. This should be in the context of the setting where the child engages in routine interactions and activities on a daily basis. Adjustments need to occur regularly as indicated by the results of monitoring the child's progress.

375. If significant changes are needed in a child's program for which there is an IEP, designated members of the child's team will need to convene. Parents and early childhood educators, child care providers, or teachers need to have input regarding the changes needed and to be clearly informed of what the changes will be.

376. There are many sensitive issues that challenge parents with children having special needs. Educators need to be alert to these and to be honest with parents about their concerns regarding the child. However, at the same time, it is important to be supportive of the needs of the parents and be aware of their level of sensitivity. Acknowledge and encourage the effort, love, patience, and care that the parents extend to their child.

377. When checking the progress of the children in your group, be aware of the limitations some children with special needs have regarding the demonstration of what they know through traditional assessment techniques. For these children, either use alternate assessment techniques or make the decision not to assess the child at this point. Discuss this with the child's parents and other members on the child's IEP team.

378. For children who have more severe disabilities, be especially selective in what assessment tools you use. Assistive devices may be needed for these children to better demonstrate what they know and can do. For these children, the observations of parents and teachers along with informal measures of functional levels may be the most useful for programming purposes.

379. The National Association for the Education of Young Children (NAEYC) has published an excellent position paper regarding the assessment of children with special needs. This paper can be found in Wolery and Wilbers (1994), *Including Children with Special Needs in Early Childhood Programs.* This book is a must for your library if you are working with children with special needs.

SUMMARY

Assessment is an ongoing process when working with young children. Being informed about the latest and best assessment practices is the responsibility of all adults who work with children in all school settings. This will ensure that assessments are always done with the best interests of the child in mind.

Children with developmental delays and disabilities will need to be assessed far more frequently and more critically than children without special needs. Adults who are sensitive to the needs of children, are knowledgeable about child development, and understand and love children for who they are can make these assessments a positive experience for children and their parents.

10

Learning in the
21st Century

We live in a rapidly changing world. Do our present curricula, instructional methods, and beliefs meet the needs of children and society in the context of the 21st century? Information is presently bombarding us from many different sources at a rapid rate. Our ability to function at this pace is no longer just dependent upon how many facts we know, but also on our ability to scan a broad array of information at any given time and choose which pieces fit into the "big picture" of what is needed. This requires problem-solving capacities that are based on a holistic processing approach as well as a linear approach.

To meet the demands, learners in preschool through high school will need to be given experiences and taught skills that will reflect this methodology. This requires a shift in our educational practices, which formerly emphasized a linear approach to learning and problem solving, the memorization of facts rather than learning how to access information, and the reliance on external resources without an equal consideration given to one's inner resources. Even though these approaches may have served us well in the past, they are decreasing in effectiveness to serve us in meeting the demands of our information age and global society. Acknowledging the need for change in our current educational (and parenting) practices is the first step in moving forward.

The next step will require us to assess the changes that have taken place in children, the changes in society, the changes in understanding how children learn, and how to support children in the learning process. Data obtained from research about how the brain learns, knowledge of the application of new technologies to education, and a better understanding of the part emotions, nutrition, and the environment play in learning can provide the structure for evaluating and implementing the necessary changes.

HOW THE BRAIN LEARNS

The results of some of the new techniques used in brain research are providing more and more information about the organization and functioning of brain regions serving learning, language, social competence, and ability to pay attention. This is giving us new insights into the understanding of learning and attention problems resulting in new ways of addressing these challenges when working with children. However, the application of this knowledge is being extended to children on a limited basis at this point in time. More children will benefit in their learning environments once educators take it upon themselves to connect with this new knowledge, understand it, and apply it to the teaching process.

In the current literature regarding how the brain learns, a number of ideas occur repeatedly. These can be summarized as follows:

- The brain learns best when the left (more logical and analytic) and right (more spatial, creative, and intuitive) hemispheres of the brain are engaged in the learning process.
- Learning by making connections between and among ideas and facts within the appropriate context is a more effective way for the brain to learn than by processing facts in isolation.
- The brain responds well to novelty and input that is varied and uses as many senses as possible.
- Learning is most effective when the participant is actively engaged as opposed to passively listening or watching.
- The more relevant educational material is to a child's life, the better he will remember it.
- Positive emotions paired with learning experiences produce greater success in learning.
- Immediate feedback helps the brain reinforce its neural pathways of information and responses.
- Learning occurs best in a stimulating, nonthreatening environment that incorporates positive emotional support and a sense of fun and exploration.
- Learning is most effective when input is provided at a level of difficulty that is appropriate for each child at his functional and developmental level.
- Learning is encouraged when a child is given choices and a degree of control.
- For optimum stability and effectiveness, a child needs a broad range of skills and interests that are mental, physical, emotional, aesthetic, and social.
- The brain and the rest of the body need to be supported with a diet that supplies adequate protein, complex carbohydrates, "healthy" fats, vitamins, minerals, and calories.

New findings from neuroscience and other scientific research are continually adding to our knowledge to help us understand how the brain learns. Authors and educators such as Eric Jensen, David Sousa, Pat Wolfe, and Robert Sylwester have provided the educational community with excellent books about the brain and how to apply these in teaching children (see References and Recommended Reading for specific titles).

MIND/BODY/HEART INTERDEPENDENCE

Children need adequate amounts of rest and sleep for the mind/body/heart to grow and develop the structures necessary for learning. In our fast-paced society, this need is often not met. This can result in states of imbalance in children of all ages. Associated behaviors of this imbalance can be observed as irritability, lack of motivation and concentration, and memory difficulties. Sleep is needed not only for the body to rebuild itself but also for information learned to be transferred to long-term memory. Rest in the form of "downtime" and relaxation is necessary to balance the high levels of activity in which children engage.

In today's society, children need to feel an increased sense of physical and psychological safety. With an increase in violence and bullying in our schools and communities along with the continued reminders about terrorism, we need to pay more attention to this issue. Attention can be given in the form of emotional support for children who are directly affected as well as for those children who are fearful in their various environments. All adults need to continue to work on ways to provide safer environments for children so their learning, emotional well-being, and physical condition are not compromised by their psychological or physical fears.

Recent brain research is helping to explain how movement directly benefits the nervous system. It has been found that muscular activities, particularly coordinated movements, appear to stimulate the production of neurotrophins, natural substances, that stimulate the growth of nerve cells and increases the number of neural connections in the brain. The number of neural connections and subsequent networks directly impact learning by integrating and anchoring new information and experience into these neural networks. Movement helps to awaken and activate many of our mental capacities, which in turn increase learning and creativity. In addition, movement can also help release tension, which results in better stress management. Knowledge of this type needs to be shared with all adults who live or work with children so that physical exercise and all forms of movement are an integral part of each child's day.

Evidence from brain science supports the need to pay more attention to the part that emotions play in the learning process. According to researchers such as Paul MacLean, Director of the Laboratory of Brain Evolution and Behavior at the National Institute of Mental Health in Bethesda, Maryland; Daniel Goleman, author of *Emotional Intelligence: Why It Can Matter More Than IQ*; and researchers at the Institute of HeartMath in Boulder Creek, California, emotions are vital to thinking processes.

Psychiatrist William Gray has proposed a model of the mind that says that "ideas are rooted in emotional codes," which he calls "feeling tones." These tones, according to his model, serve as vehicles through which rational ideas are remembered, associated, and reported. Does this mean that children may get more out of *how* something is being taught rather than from *what* is being taught (the content of the curriculum)? This whole area needs to be explored further relative to how the brain learns and its implications for learning.

Knowledge about the mind/body/heart interdependence has expanded our options for working with all children. It also gives us new insights for working with children with special needs. For example, medication and self-management techniques have been the primary treatments for children diagnosed with an ADHD or ADD disorder. Even though much success has been achieved through the use of neurofeedback, diet, movement, and auditory stimulation programs, these approaches have been used on a limited basis by parents and educators.

NUTRITION AND LEARNING

In the past decade there has been a significant increase in the number of children who are considered to be obese. Simultaneously, there has also been an increase in type 2 diabetes among children, which is thought to be linked to obesity. The number of children this affects has now become a national concern. There are both short- and long-term compromises to children's health, learning, and behavior as this trend continues. We are clearly at a point where this issue needs to be addressed at all levels locally and nationally.

The scientific and nutritional communities have made us more aware of the relationship between what we eat and the corresponding responses of our physical bodies. In educational circles, we have not paid enough attention to the effect of diet on mental clarity, memory functions, concentration, and behavior. The present concern regarding learning, attention, and behavior problems in our nation's preschool and school settings warrants a closer look at this issue. This needs to be done from two perspectives: the accessing of knowledge about the relationship between diet and the brain, and a dialogue about how this knowledge can be applied by educators and parents to assist with the learning process and with the behavior of children.

Since preschool settings and primary grades provide the first structured basis for children's learning, it is critical for young children and for all children who are biochemically more vulnerable (i.e., who respond more negatively to inadequate nutrition) than other children to receive the most nutritious foods available.

Recent studies regarding the relationship between nutrition and learning suggest that many children who have difficulty learning or attention difficulties often have specific nutritional deficits. Correcting these deficits in some children has resulted in increased learning performance and concentration, which in turn concurrently impact the behavior of children. In some cases, the identified problem no longer exists.

It is important that all children get adequate amounts of protein, complex carbohydrates, essential fatty acids, vitamins, and minerals in their daily diets. When one or more of these essential elements are lacking for a period of time, learning and behavior are compromised.

An often overlooked requirement of the body and brain is its need for a continuous supply of water. Children need to be given the opportunity to have access to water bottles in their various environments throughout the day. Studies have shown that the learning and behavior of children benefit from well-hydrated bodies and brains.

Schools play a vital role in educating children (and their parents when needed) about the importance of eating healthy foods. A point to begin this process can be through the school lunch program. Examples of school districts that have been innovative in creating healthy lunch programs include Berkeley, California; Chicago, Illinois (inner-city school lunch program); and Appleton, Wisconsin.

RESPONSIBILITY

Young children initially learn through imitation and interaction. Parents or parental figures are the first models children experience through observation and interaction. Translated to all learning environments for children, this means that adults who choose to work with young children take on the responsibility for modeling the types of social interactions and enthusiasm for learning that we want young children to imitate.

In addition to this, we are also responsible for providing a foundation of learning that will serve them well throughout their school years and beyond. To do this is going to take some serious consideration on our part as to what type of models we need to create for children and how these can connect them with who they are within the context of society. To do this, we need to give consideration to the following ideas.

When our emotional, social, intuitive, thinking, and physical selves are in balance, we feel better and are more effective at what we do. Young children are dependent upon adults to have their needs met in a holistic way that addresses all of their needs. We need to assess how we are attending to the emotional, mental, and physical dimensions for children in the home, school, and community environments. Overemphasizing one at the expense of diminishing another contributes to a state of imbalance. This compromises children's learning and general well-being. For a further discussion of the meaning of balance and activities to a balanced way of being refer to Moore (2005), *Creating Balance in Children's Lives: A Natural Approach to Learning and Behavior*, and Moore and Henrikson (2005), *Creating Balance in Children: Activities to Optimize Learning and Behavior* (see References and Recommended Reading).

There are several child development theorists and spokespersons that are worthy of consideration in developing philosophies and best practices for working with young children. We need to look for concepts that are in the best interests of children and for those that operate from an integrated approach representing a compilation of thought. No one philosophy, belief system, or conceptual framework can serve all children equally well. Theorists such as Piaget, Vgotsky, Erikson, and Steiner (to name a few) have made major contributions to understanding and developing programs for young children. Paired with this information should be the knowledge parents, educators, and other adults have accumulated through their direct experiences of being and working with children.

The more we pay attention to our own evolution as adults, the more we can create programs that honor the evolutionary process for children. As a part of this process, we need to look at new ways of expanding and applying the concept of viewing the child as an interaction of mind, body, and heart. As adults, we need to think, feel, and act from a position of "wholeness," fully recognizing the interdependent nature of these three dimensions.

Curricula based on the routine life experiences of children, their interests, and their developmental readiness need to be evaluated relative to our current practices. We need to ask ourselves the question, "Does placing too much emphasis on the learning of letters, words, and numbers while ignoring children's natural interests and readiness deter their joy and enthusiasm for learning?" This is not an either/or issue, but one of balancing elements of both that are consistent with developmentally appropriate practices and a "whole child" perspective.

Legislation, research, experience, and court decisions support the rights of all children to have equal access to any program and setting. Equal access means that all child care centers, preschool settings, and school settings accept children along a continuum of learning and behavior reflecting a variety of developmental patterns and abilities. Are we doing what we need to do in implementing this right for all children?

As we make the commitment to do this, we will meet challenges. In working these through, we need to ask ourselves the question, "Are our choices for curriculum, materials, and methodology appropriate for the child?" rather than "What is wrong with the child?"

How do we model and teach toward a balance of what is in the best interest of the individual within the context of community? First, we need to discover what this balance is in various situations and environments. Second, we need to determine the elements to consider in reaching this balance. Then, we need to model the behaviors that embrace a balance for both the individual and the group so that children can imitate our behaviors and eventually take on this practice themselves.

We need to use our hearts to help guide us, putting a combination of feelings and thoughts into action as we work with each other and with children. The unconditional love we give to young children will mirror itself exponentially. Options for bringing positive energy and creativity into learning are clearly present if we work toward integrating the heart and the mind.

Young children are the products of the present and the harbingers of the future. Can we afford not to extend these gifts to all children equally in ways that support them for who they are? The evolution of learning needed for all children within the context of the 21st century is dependent upon our willingness, creativity, and success in moving forward. As stated by an unknown author, "If not me, who? If not now, when?"

Appendix A

Forms and Activities

Form 1   Profile of Development

Name of Child: _____ Date: _____

		A	R	E	A	S
		Chronological Age	Language Development	Large Motor Development	Social Development	Cognitive Development
D E V E L O P M E N T A L A G E	6					
	5.5					
	5					
	4.5					
	4					
	3.5					
	3					
	2.5					
	2					
	1.5					
	1					

See Figure 1.3 for a completed example.

Form 2   Cycles of Learning

Example: Preparatory Writing

Awareness Phase: Create a learning center or set aside a space in your room where you can display a variety of shapes, letters, and words in different color media. Provide writing tools, paper, sand trays, paintbrushes, and watercolors for the children to experiment with in making shapes and letters.

Exploratory Phase: Assign small groups (no more than four at a time) to the designated area. Encourage them to become acquainted with the shapes and letters by tracing around them with their hands. Then have them experiment with making their own shapes and letters with the materials you have provided.

Inquiry Phase: Have children share their experiences with you. Ask the children questions about what they have learned. Supplement the children's information by sharing with them other information about letters.

Application: Discuss uses of the shapes from which letters are made. Show how you can make names, signs, and so forth by combining certain letters. Provide the children with an experience through which they can make their names or signs to put up in their rooms at home. Children who cannot use writing tools can make their name (at least the first letter) from clay or play dough.

Note: This same format can be used for introducing children to new experiences, concepts, skills, and so forth in any area of interest. To facilitate this process, you may wish to have several blank forms available upon which to write plans. Make it useful for you. On the next page is an example of a format that can be used.

Form 2 (Continued)

Topic: _____   Date: _____

Purpose:

Materials needed:

Awareness Phase:

Exploration Phase:

Inquiry Phase:

Application Phase:

Comments regarding success of activity:

Changes I would make the next time I do this:

Form 3   Behavior as a Function of the Interaction of the Child and His Environment

Behavior is the result of an interactive process that takes place between a child and his environment. What the child brings to a situation, event, or relationship, and what happens as a result of the interaction influences future behavior. Portrayed visually, it appears as follows:

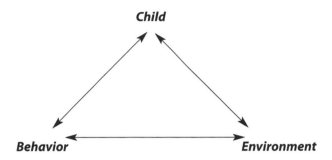

Example of Factors in Each Component:

Child	Environment	Behavior
• Strengths	• Supporting, caring, and loving adults	• Well-adjusted
• Limitations	• Dysfunctional adults	• Aggressive
• Temperament	• Transitions/change	• Withdrawn
• Interests	• Trauma	• Fearful
• Vulnerabilities	• Experiences/events	• Caring
• Personality	• Societal expectations	• Affectionate
• Genetic	• Subculture values	• Learns easily
• Predisposition	• Environmental conditions	• Difficulty learning
	• Nutrition	

Note: Words placed horizontally are not related across columns

    To gain a better understanding of a child, use the information on this form plus what you add to each column to create a format for assessing the areas you need to further explore.

Form 4   General Strategies for Working With Young Children

Directions: Several strategies are listed below. Place two checks on the blank in front of the ones you are currently using. Place one check in the blank space for the ones you wish to try. After a period of two weeks, circle the numbers of the strategies that have been most effective for the child with whom you are working and continue to use them.

Child's Name: _____   Date: _____

_____ 1. Expectations for performance are consistent with the child's development and cognitive abilities. If not, revise your expectations.

_____ 2. Allow more time for the child to get ready and complete his activities.

_____ 3. Provide a quiet area where the child can go when needed.

_____ 4. Provide special seating when in a small or large group activity.

_____ 5. Filter out excessive noise or distracting sounds for the child when needed.

_____ 6. Adjust the kind and amount of lighting for the child.

_____ 7. Talk to the child's parents about the eating and sleeping patterns of the child.

_____ 8. Try the use of color for calming and concentration when needed.

_____ 9. Try adding music while the child is engaged in certain activities.

_____10. List additional strategies you wish to try.

Form 5   Categories of Modifications

Directions: Select one or more of the categories listed below that you wish to try for a specific child or small group of children. Under each category, list the interventions that you will implement. After the intervention has been used several times, mark the degree of effectiveness of the modification.

Child's Name: _____   Date: _____

Category 1: Adjust the demands of the activity. List the methods you will use to accomplish this, such as shorten the number of items to complete, use checklists instead of having a child write sentences, and so forth.

_____

_____

_____

_____

Circle the degree of effectiveness:

Very   Satisfactory   Not Effective

Continue the modification?   *With changes*

Yes   Yes/No

Category 2: Preteach the skills needed for the activity. List the skills needed for the activity.

_____

_____

_____

_____

Circle the degree of effectiveness:

Very   Satisfactory   Not Effective

Continue the modification?   *With changes*

Yes   Yes/No

Category 3: Modify the expected outcome of the activity for the child. List the modified outcome(s) for this child.

_____

_____

_____

_____

(Continued)

Form 5 (Continued)

Circle the degree of effectiveness:

Very   Satisfactory   Not Effective

Continue the modification?   *With changes*

Yes   Yes/No

Category 4: Provide an adult or peer (circle one) who will assist the child while doing the activity. List the assistance that will be given to the child.

_____

_____

_____

_____

Circle the degree of effectiveness:

Very   Satisfactory   Not Effective

Continue the modification?   *With changes*

Yes   Yes/No

Category 5: Plan a parallel activity for the child to do while the other children are engaged in the assigned activity. Make the parallel activity as similar as possible. Describe the parallel activity you will use.

_____

_____

_____

_____

Circle the degree of effectiveness:

Very   Satisfactory   Not Effective

Continue the modification?   *With changes*

Yes   Yes/No

Note: You may wish to combine modifications such as adjusting the activity and providing assistance. Keep these sheets as documentation of the modifications you have made for a specific child. After you have done this process with several children, make a compiled list of all the successful modifications for future use with other children who need modifications in similar circumstances. After a year or more you will have an invaluable resource. Teachers who work with similar ages or grade levels can combine their lists of modifications to share with each other.

Form 6   Creating a Personal Dictionary of Familiar Objects

Steps in Creating a Personal Dictionary:

1. Provide the child with several pages of blank paper bound with a plastic spiral or some other form of binding.

2. Have the child choose the color of the paper he wants in his dictionary.

3. Have the child personalize the dictionary by having him decorate the outside cover.

4. Divide the pages of the dictionary into several sections. Start by having one page for each entry.

5. Start with the categories of common objects at school, favorite toys, favorite animals, and favorite objects at home. Add to these categories as the child is ready.

6. Present each object in the following sequence:

   ○ Give the child the object to look at, feel, and hold.

   ○ For favorite animals, use stuffed toy animals.

   ○ Have the child tell you as much as he can about the object. If he cannot tell you in words, have him demonstrate the use of the object with the object itself when possible, or have him show you by gestures or pantomime.

   ○ Show the child a picture of the object while the child is holding the object. Use pictures that are cut and ready for pasting in the child's dictionary. Use words cut out of magazines that can be used as labels for the pictures in the dictionary, or write out the labels yourself.

   ○ Tell the child the name of the object.

   ○ Draw a rectangle on the piece of paper.

   ○ Have the child paste the picture and name for each object into his dictionary.

   ○ Present the child with a new object, picture, and label each day, repeating the same sequence of steps.

   ○ Each day when the child adds a new object to his dictionary, review the previous entries so that the child can build on his vocabulary, his recognition skills, and his understanding of common objects and their associated names in printed form.

Note: There can be many variations on this process, such as using actions instead of objects, or varying the amount of work the child does independently or with assistance. This is an excellent project in which to involve parents or volunteers from the community.

Directions: When working with young children, have them start out with very simple mazes before progressing to more difficult ones. When the children get familiar with how mazes work, have them create mazes for each other. Make a collection of these mazes so children can choose which ones they want to use. The child who created the maze will feel a sense of accomplishment and satisfaction through the recognition of having created something for others.

Draw by hand two horizontal parallel lines about six inches long (see below). Place the pictures of two objects, animals, trees, or people at points A and B. Here is an example of this simple maze:

Encourage children to stay within the lines if possible.

Next, instead of two parallel straight lines, create your maze with wavy lines:

Next, combine parallel vertical lines with parallel horizontal lines to make the maze more complex:

Keep adding lines and varying the shapes of the mazes as the children become proficient at the increasing complexity of the mazes. Some samples follow:

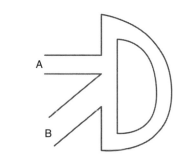

Form 8   Learning About Feelings Through Working With Animals

Directions: Ask the children in your group to tell you what kind of pets they have at home. For children who do not have pets, ask them what their favorite animal is. Make a list of all the animals the children name. Lead the children in a discussion about how different animals show that they are happy, sad, excited, tired, mad, scared, and lovable. Compare the feelings animals show to the feelings children express by creating a chart with the expressions of the feelings of each type of animal. An example follows.

Sample Expression of Feelings Chart

Feeling	Child	Animal
Happy	Smile	Dog—Wags tail Cat—Purrs Bird—Sings
Excited	Talks fast Gestures/body movements	Dog—Barks Cat—Tail moves back and forth Bird—Chatters
Tired	Yawns, sleeps	Dog—Sleeps Cat—Sleeps Bird—Rests, sleeps

Continue this process until you have included all the animals named that can be fit into each of the feeling categories. Be sure each animal on the list fits into some feeling category. You can add to the feelings list as the children come up with new feeling words.

You can extend this exercise to talk about the qualities (other than feelings) of each animal. To make this more meaningful to the children, have them also think of the qualities they have and which animals have similar qualities.

Depending on the age and abilities of the children you are working with, you can further extend this activity by having children draw their animal, write or dictate a few sentences about it, make up stories combining a number of animals, and so forth.

Form 9   Sharing and Talking About Feelings

Directions: Sitting on the floor in a circle formation is usually the best for this exercise. Introduce the idea of feelings children have by reading a story in which several feelings of the characters are shared through both pictures and words. List the feelings identified through the story. For each feeling listed, choose one child to draw a face expressing this feeling next to the feeling word. Then discuss with the children what it is like to feel this way, what makes them feel this way, and how they behave when this happens to them.

The second time you do this activity, introduce the idea of a talking stick. Explain to the children that only the one holding the talking stick can speak; everyone else must listen to that person without interrupting him. When the child is finished talking, he puts the stick into the middle of the circle, to be picked up by the next person to speak. The topic for this session should be a follow-up of the first session by having children share times when they had one or more of the feelings from the original list. Then have children add any new feelings they have experienced, following the same format as in the first session. As children become more comfortable with this process, have the talking stick move around the circle to each child, allowing a child to "pass" if he does not wish to share anything.

This exercise should be used on a weekly basis at least. It will help children get in touch with their feelings, share them, and talk about ways to change uncomfortable feelings into more positive feelings.

New ideas about events, situations, and associated feelings should be introduced to children from time to time to continue expanding their understanding and expression of feelings. For example, a session could be created around the dreams children have and the associated feelings that they engender.

Bring color, music, and texture into sharing sessions as a way of helping children increase their awareness of how various stimuli in our environment affect their feelings. For example, with color, bring in several colors (paper, cloth, carpet pieces, etc.) and have the children look at and feel each color. Then have them share the feelings they had while looking and feeling each of the colors. Do the same with music by having them listen to different types of music to see which makes them feel calm, energetic, and so forth. For textures, bring in rough and smooth sandpaper, rough and smooth rocks, different pieces of cloth, plastic shipping bubbles, and so on, and have them experience each through touch, describing the associated feeling.

Form 10 Learning About Feelings Through Dramatic Play

Directions: Create a list of situations that parallel the experiences of the ages of the children with whom you work. Examples of these include

- ✓ having fun with a friend

- ✓ playing with a pet

- ✓ falling down and hurting himself

- ✓ hugging a parent

- ✓ losing a game

- ✓ getting sent to his room

- ✓ going to the zoo

- ✓ getting into an argument

- ✓ getting pushed or hit by another child

- ✓ being called a name by another child

- ✓ having a birthday party

- ✓ someone accidentally breaking his toy

- ✓ a baby brother or sister being born

- ✓ losing a pet

- ✓ going on a trip

Start out by having children use puppets to role-play these situations. When doing this, it is a good practice to pair a situation with positive feelings and one with negative feelings so that children can experience the full range of feelings. When children are comfortable with using puppets for role-playing, have them volunteer play the roles themselves in each situation. Always allow enough time for children to process their feelings and think of new ways of expressing the various feelings that surface. Personalize the discussion as much as possible to fit the experiences of the children and their readiness to talk about them.

Use this activity periodically on an ongoing basis, encouraging children to add situations as they experience them in their lives, so they can continually expand upon their knowledge, their understanding of feelings, and their ability to express them.

Form 11 Learning About Empathy

Directions: It is often easier to help children experience what it is like to take the perspective of another child by first having them connect with the qualities and feelings of animals. The following exercise is one way to help children do this. Start out by choosing one animal and asking the question, "What would it feel like to be a_____?" Finish the question by filling in an animal's name and what the animal is doing.

For example:

What would it feel like to be a bird flying high up in the sky? On a calm day? On a windy day? When it is raining or snowing?

What would it feel like to be a fish swimming in the ocean? A goldfish swimming in a fishbowl?

What would it feel like to be a deer walking in the woods? A mother deer walking with its fawn?

What would it feel like to be a dog living with a happy family? A sad family?

What would it feel like to be a hamster living in a cage?

What would it feel like to be an elephant performing in a circus? Walking down the street in a parade? Walking in the jungle?

As children become familiar with this process, let them add animals and situations. Personalize this experience by having the children create situations involving other children and adults rather than animals. Use dramatic play to help children role-play a simulated experience. This brings feelings to the next level of understanding for children so that they can begin to feel empathy for other children and adults.

Form 12   Settling Conflicts Peacefully

Directions: Young children can learn to settle their conflicts when we give them a structure in which to do so. The use of a place designated as a "peace table" (you could use a beanbag instead) is one way to provide a structure for children to settle their differences. This approach generally consists of two components.

Component 1: A designated place that is kept specifically for children to use when they have a conflict with another child. Once the purpose of this place is explained to the children, have them help you name it. Make a special sign for this place.

Component 2: Guidelines for behaving at the designated peace place and steps to follow for resolving conflicts should be clearly posted. For young children who cannot read words, use pictures to convey this information.

AN EXAMPLE OF GUIDELINES

- ✓ Use quiet voices while in this area.
- ✓ Keep your hands and feet to yourself.
- ✓ Be as calm as you can when talking to the other child.
- ✓ Only one group of children can be in the area at a time and are not to be disturbed by other children.
- ✓ Let the children think up ideas to add.

An example of steps to use in settling conflicts peacefully follows:

1. Use a spinner to determine which child will talk first (whichever child is closest to the direction where the spinner is pointing). The child who is not speaking needs to listen until the child speaking has finished what he needs to say. You may wish to use the "talking stick" idea for this process to help children remember that they can only speak when they are holding the stick.

2. Each child needs to take a turn in explaining what happened and how it made him feel.

3. Each child needs to respond to what the other child said.

4. Both children need to agree to end the disagreement or conflict between them.

5. Each child needs to offer one suggestion as to how they can avoid getting into a conflict if this happens again.

The above components are offered as a way to begin this type of conflict resolution. It will need to be modified and adjusted, depending upon the ages of the children and the types of conflicts they have. In any case, initiating such a structure will take several practice sessions with adult supervision for children to resolve their issues successfully on their own.

Form 13   Steps for Problem Solving

The following steps for problem solving may be used with a single child or with a group of children. Once this process has been taught and used, children will begin to use it independently or with only a slight reminder. Have the child

1. tell what the problem is; if the child does not know how to describe the problem in words, have him find a picture that tells or suggests what the problem is, or have him draw one;

2. tell how having the problem makes him feel; again, if the words are not there, encourage the child to find a picture or refer to the feelings chart (which you should have in your room);

3. tell you what he did about the problem; brainstorm other ways of solving the problem (you should add your ideas also);

4. choose one thing to do to solve the problem and tell you when he is going to try it; encourage him to try it as soon as possible;

5. tell you what the outcome of his actions from number 4 were as soon as he completes the action; if the child is successful, celebrate; if not, go back to number 3 and have the child choose a different action to take.

Providing children the skills and practice to solve problems helps children become more independent and feel better about themselves. This helps children to lay the foundation for relying on their own resources rather than external ones.

Form 14 Steps in Changing Behavior

1. Identify the behavior you wish to change either to decrease a problem behavior or increase a positive behavior. Pinpoint the behavior by being as specific as possible, (i.e., hitting peers during play or at snack times).

2. Write down the goal you wish to achieve. For example, a short-term goal would be to decrease the number of hitting behaviors towards peers during play or snack time. A long-term goal would be to eliminate these behaviors.

3. List the steps you need to reach the goal (i.e., decreasing the hitting behaviors during snack times, decreasing the behaviors during playtimes, eliminating hitting behaviors during snack or playtimes). Reaching a goal via several small steps is usually more successful than attempting to achieve a goal in a single step, especially for young children.

4. Establish a baseline (how often the behavior occurs now) by counting the frequency of the behavior during snack or playtimes for a period of three to four consecutive days. Record the frequency on a chart that is easily accessible. Golf counters work well for charting the frequency of behaviors.

5. Decide on the method and type of chart you will use for recording the behavior you are attempting to change. Determine the consequences (activity, social, or material reinforcer) that will help bring about the desired change.

6. Evaluate the effectiveness of your behavior management program by recording the child's frequency of targeted behavior over the set period of time. Then determine if there is a decrease in frequency compared to the frequency of these behaviors recorded on your original baseline. If the behavior is decreasing in frequency, your methods and consequences are appropriate. If not, you need to go back to Step 5 and make changes.

For an example of a chart to use for recording the frequency of a child's behaviors, see Form 15.

Form 15   Charting Frequency of Targeted Behaviors

Directions: Record the frequency of a behavior you wish to change by recording the number of times a behavior occurs within a defined time period before an intervention is initiated.

Behavior Frequency Chart

Child's Name: _____   Date: _____

Behavior: _____

Date	Activity	Time Interval	Number of Behaviors

If the targeted behavior you observed and recorded is excessive relative to similar age peers in the same activity, plan an appropriate intervention to decrease the behavior.

Interventions can include social or material reinforcers, a token system, consequences such as lost privileges, or any other intervention that is appropriate.

Form 16   Charting Effect of Interventions

Directions: Record the frequency of a child's behaviors from Form 15 in the column labeled *Baseline Frequency.* Then begin recording the frequency of a child's behavior in the second column when you start the intervention.

Behavior Frequency Chart

Child's Name: _____   Date: _____

Targeted Behavior: _____

		Baseline Frequency			*Frequency of Behaviors With Intervention*								
F 30 X													
R 25 X													
E 20 X													
Q													
U 15 X													
E 10 X													
N													
C 5 X													
Y	1	2	3	4	1	2	3	4	5	6	7	8	9
					Day								

After about five days of the using the intervention, note if the targeted behavior (the behavior you wish to change) is changing in the direction you wish. If the intervention is working, continue the intervention until the targeted behavior reaches an appropriate level. If the behavior does not change, make note of it and create a different intervention. Repeat the process as needed.

Form 17   Child Observation Form

Directions: Record behaviors as they occur. To make this type of observation, use the following steps:

1. Choose the activity that you wish to observe the child doing.

2. Place yourself in full sight of the child but not next to the child. If you are supervising the activity or leading the activity, carry a small note pad and pencil with you.

3. Write down what the child is doing when you start the observation (i.e., participating with the others, off by himself, etc.). See the form for recording the child's behaviors on the next page.

4. Every time you observe behaviors that are specific to the child (where no other child is demonstrating this behavior), record the time and note what the child did.

5. Continue doing this until the activity is completed. When the activity is completed, record the time and the outcome of the activity for the child.

6. Analyze the data.

(Continued)

Form for Recording Behaviors as They Occur

Child's Name: _____   Date: _____

Observation Done by: _____   Position: _____

Activity Observed: _____

Time	Behavior
etc.	etc.—Add as many lines as needed

Analysis of Data:

✓ Number of minutes the activity lasted:

✓ Number of "different" behaviors observed:

✓ Number of times a "different" behavior occurred:

✓ The most frequently observed behavior was:

✓ List any patterns of behavior that emerged and label them positive or negative depending upon the effect on the child being observed or on the other children in the group.

✓ Make a note of other information you get from the data, such as the amount of time they spend on-task versus off-task.

✓ Conclusions drawn from this observation:

Form for Recording Behaviors as They Occur

Child's Name: _____   Date: _____

Observation Done by:_____   Position: _____

Activity Observed: _____

Time	Behavior

EXAMPLE 1

Observing a Child's Degree of Engagement in an Activity

Directions: After observing a child in an activity, use the following key to record the child's level of involvement in the activity.

1. The child avoids the activity or makes no attempt to become involved when an opportunity to engage in the activity is given.

2. The child attempts the activity but seeks help or support in order to do so.

3. The child engages in the activity with satisfaction.

4. The child uses a variety of skills equally well when engaging in the activity.

Child's Name: _____   Date: _____

Observed by: _____   Position: _____

Name/Type of Activity	Rating (1–4)

This is an excellent method to use in gaining information about the child's strengths, areas of interest, and areas in which he needs assistance or improvement.

EXAMPLE 2

You may want to expand on this form by extending it and using it as a means of measuring a child's progress in time intervals. The appropriate time interval for young children can be either monthly or a minimum of four times a year. If used this way, the chart would appear as follows:

Name/Type of Activity	Time Intervals		
	Date/Rating	Date/Rating	Date/Rating

This method of observing and recording young children's behavior can be adapted to fit the purpose you wish it to serve and the information you need to access.

See the complete forms for recording the behaviors you observe on the next two pages.

Form 18 (Continued)

Child's Name:_____   Date: _____

Observed by: _____   Position: _____

Name/Type of Activity	Rating (1–4)

Name/Type of Activity	Time Intervals		
	Date/Rating	Date/Rating	Date/Rating

Form 19   Interview About the Child

Child's Name: _____   Date: _____

Interview by: _____   Position: _____

How long have you known _____?

In what capacity have you known _____?

Tell me about _____'s strengths.

Tell me about _____'s limitations.

What concerns do you have regarding _____'s learning? Other areas of development?

Tell me about any health-related problems you have experienced in working with _____.

Is there anything else you wish to share about _____ that would be helpful for the people working with him or her?

Add any additional questions that you feel would be beneficial for obtaining additional information in working with the child. If you interview the child's parents, change the wording as needed. Also add a question regarding the primary language spoken at home: does the child understand and converse in any additional languages? Ask if there have been any major changes, transitions, or trauma in the child's life that would be helpful for you to know about.

Appendix B

Resources: National Organizations

American Speech-Language-Hearing Association
2200 Research Blvd.
Rockville, MD 20850
800-638-8255
www.asha.org

The Arc of the United States
1010 Wayne Avenue Suite 650
Silver Spring, MD 20910
800-433-5255
www.thearc.org

Autism Society of America
7910 Woodmont Avenue, Suite 300
Bethesda, MD 20814
800-328-8476
www.autism-society.org

Brain Connection
888-358-0212
www.brainconnection.com

Children and Adults with ADD (CHADD)
8181 Professional Place, Suite 150
Landover, MD 20785
301-306-7070
www.chadd.org

Council for Exceptional Children (CEC)
Division for Learning Disabilities
1110 North Glebe Road, Suite 300
Arlington, VA 22201
888-232-7733
www.cec.sped.org

Council for Learning Disabilities
11184 Antioch Road
Box 405
Overland Park, KS 66210
913-491-1011
www.cldinternational.org

Disability Resources Monthly
www.disabilityresources.org

Family Education Network
20 Park Plaza, 12th Floor
Boston, MA 02116
www.familyeducation.com

Federal Resource Center for Special Education
1825 Connecticut Avenue, NW
Washington, DC 20009
202-884-8215
www.rrfeenetwork.org

Federation of Families for Children's Mental Health
9605 Medical Center, Suite 280
Rockville, MD 20850
240-403-1901
www.ffcmh.org

Gesell Institute of Human Development
310 Prospect Street
New Haven, CT 06511
800-369-7709
www.gesellinstitute.org

Institute of HeartMath
3033 Moorpath Ave. #6
San Jose, CA 95128
831-338-8500
www.heartmath.org

The International Dyslexia Association
40 York Road
Baltimore, MD 21204
410-296-0232
www.interdys.org

Internet Resources for Special Children
www.irsc.org

Jensen Learning
4202 Sorrento Valley Blvd., Suite B
San Diego, CA 92121
888-638-7246
www.jensenlearning.com

LD Online
www.ldonline.com

Learning Disabilities Association of America (LDA)
4156 Library Road
Pittsburgh, PA 15234
888-300-6710
www.ldaamerica.org

National Association for the Visually Handicapped
22 West 21st Street
New York, NY 10016
212-889-3141
www.navh.org

National Center for Learning Disabilities (NCLD)
381 Park Avenue South, Suite 1420
New York, NY 10016
888-575-7373
www.ncld.org

National Dissemination Center for Children with Disabilities (NICHCY)
PO Box 1492
Washington, DC 20013
800-695-0285
www.nichcy.org

National Early Childhood Technical Assistance Center
Campus Box 8040, UNC-CH
Chapel Hill, NC 27599
www.nectac.org

School Psychology Resources Online
www.schoolpsychology.net

Schwab Learning
1650 South Amphlett Blvd #300
San Mateo, CA 94402
650-655-2410
www.schwablearning.org

Special Education Resources on the Internet
www.seriweb.com

TASH
1025 Vermont Avenue, NW, 7th Floor
Washington, DC 20005
202-263-5600
www.tash.org

Appendix C

Glossary

The words contained in this glossary are defined in the context in which they are found in this book. They are not meant to be complete definitions.

achievement: An accomplishment in learning or in the completion of a project.

age-equivalent score: A score based on the average performance of children at a particular age level; expressed as a numerical value, first by year and then by month of a child's age.

assessment: Using informal techniques such as observation and formal techniques such as standardized tests to document what a child can do or what he knows.

attending behaviors: Focusing and paying attention to a person, event, or task.

behavior: The visible expression and actions of a child.

behavior management plan: A plan of action prescribed for a specific child to decrease inappropriate behaviors or increase appropriate behaviors for a given situation.

brain balancing: Using techniques or activities that engage the functions associated with both hemispheres of the brain simultaneously.

children with special needs: Children with identified and documented disabilities or developmental delays.

cognitive ability: Intelligence; one's proficiency in problem solving; one's capacity to think or to learn.

collaboration: A team effort based on the idea of working together effectively and providing mutual emotional, mental, and physical support for one another.

cycles of learning: A four-phase recurring cycle that includes awareness, exploration, inquiry, and utilization and provides the foundation for the planning and implementation of learning experiences.

developmentally appropriate practice: Educational practices that encompass both age appropriateness and individual appropriateness.

distractibility/distraction: The result of being easily influenced by external stimuli (such as visible objects, people, and sound) that take one's focus away from the task at hand.

hyperactivity: Excessive activity in relation to others of the same age and in similar situations, often expressed as nonstop body movements or excessive verbalization.

IDEA: See Individuals with Disabilities Education Act.

IEP: See individual educational plan.

inclusion: The practice of providing learning experiences for children with special needs in the same setting as children without special needs.

individual educational plan (IEP): A written plan for the educational program of a child with special needs. This plan is developed by the local school in collaboration with preschool programs, early childhood programs, and K–12 school programs. Development and implementation of this plan must be in accordance with rules developed by the state the child resides in and federal guidelines. An IEP is written for a 12-month period and must be reviewed and revised annually.

Individuals with Disabilities Education Act (IDEA): The federal law governing education for children with special needs, formerly Education for All Handicapped Children Act.

learning: Any experience that results in a change of behavior.

learning disability: Having a condition defined by IDEA that adversely affects a child's learning performance.

least restrictive environment (LRE): The practice of placing a child with special needs in the least restrictive environment, in most cases at the school they would normally attend and in a regular education classroom.

mental image: The picture created in one's head to represent a word, symbol, or experience.

mistaken behavior: Behavior that a child engages in that is inappropriate for the situation.

modifications: Adaptations made in the curriculum, activities, presentation method, or environment to provide support for the individual child to be successful.

motor development: The growth of large and small muscles in the body needed to perform tasks involving movement of the various body parts, eye movements, and eye/hand coordination.

percentile score: A standardized score that tells how a child scored compared to other children. This score tells how many children (expressed as a percentile) scored above and below a particular child's score.

psychological processing: Mental functions involved with taking in information, organizing it, transforming it, storing it, and using it.

specific learning disability: A condition in which a child does not adequately achieve relative to the child's age or to meet state-approved grade-level standards in one or more of the areas defined by IDEA. This discrepancy must be due to a **psychological processing** difficulty rather than environmental conditions.

standard score: A raw score (based on the number correct) that has been transformed to have a given mean (midpoint) and standard deviation from the mean. A common number used to denote the midpoint of the average range is 100 with a standard deviation of 15 points. Any test that has 100 as the midpoint and a standard deviation of 15 can be compared to another.

strategies: Techniques or tools to help one approach learning and problem solving in a systematic way.

time out: A technique used to redirect a child's behavior from inappropriate to appropriate.

verbal abilities: The understanding, manipulation, and expression of information and ideas in words.

visual-motor integration: Often referred to as eye/hand coordination. It is the act of using the eyes and small motor skills together to produce written words, symbols, and pictures.

visual-spatial abilities: The understanding and manipulation of material presented through the use of pictures, symbols, and models while also responding to their spatial placement.

"whole child" perspective: Recognizing the inner world of the child and addressing the physical, emotional, social, and intuitive needs of the child in a balanced way.

References and Recommended Reading

Baker, B. L., & Brightman, A. J. (1989). *Steps to independence: A skills training guide for parents and teachers of children with special needs* (2nd ed.). Baltimore, MD: Paul H. Brooks.

Beaty, J. J. (1992). *Observing development of the young child* (3rd ed.). New York: Macmillan.

Berk, L. E., & Winsler, A. (1995). *Scaffolding children's learning: Vygotsky and early childhood education.* Washington, DC: National Association for the Education of Young Children.

Bock, K., & Stauth, C. (2007). *Healing the new childhood epidemics: Autism, ADHD, asthma, and allergies.* New York: Ballantine Books.

Bredekamp, S. (Ed.). (1987). *Developmentally appropriate practice in early childhood programs serving children from birth through age 8.* Washington, DC: National Association for the Education of Young Children.

Bredekamp, S., & Rosegrant, T. (Eds.). (1992). *Reaching potentials: Appropriate curriculum and assessment for young children* (Vol. 1). Washington, DC: National Association for the Education of Young Children.

Burns, L. (2002). *The sixth sense of children: Nurturing your child's intuitive abilities.* New York: New American Library.

Campbell, D. (2000). *The Mozart effect for children: Awakening your child's mind, health, and creativity with music.* New York: HarperCollins.

Carroll, L., & Tober, J. (1999). *The indigo children: The new kids have arrived.* Carlsbad, CA: Hay House.

Chandler, P. A. (1994). *A place for me: Including children with special needs in early care and education settings.* Washington, DC: National Association for the Education of Young Children.

Chenfeld, M. B. (1993). *Teaching in the key of life.* Washington, DC: National Association for the Education of Young Children.

Childre, D. L. (1996). *Teaching children to love: 80 games & fun activities for raising balanced children in unbalanced times.* Boulder Creek, CA: Planetary Publications.

Childre, D. L., & Martin, H. (with Beech, D.). (1999). *The HeartMath solution: The Institute of HeartMath's revolutionary program for engaging the power of the heart's intelligence.* New York: HarperCollins.

Compart, P. J., & Laake, D. (2006). *The kid-friendly ADHD and autism cookbook.* Beverly, MA: Fair Winds.

Cox, M. V. (1991). *The child's point of view: The development of cognition and language* (2nd ed.). New York: Guilford.

DeGaetano, G. D. (1993**)**. *Television and the lives of our children: A manual for teachers and parents.* Redmond, WA: Train of Thought.

Dennison, P. E., & Dennison, G. E. (1986). *Brain gym.* Ventura, CA: Edu-Kinesthetics.

Diamond, M., & Hopson, J. (1998). *Magic trees of the mind: How to nurture your child's intelligence, creativity, and healthy emotions from birth through adolescence.* New York: Penguin Putnam.

Drew, N. (1995). *Learning the skills of peacemaking: A K–6 activity guide on resolving conflict, communicating, and cooperating.* Carson, CA: Jalmar.

Eliot, L. (1999). *What's going on in there? How the brain and mind develop in the first five years of life.* New York: Bantam Books.

Elkind, D. (1993). *Images of the young child: Collected essays on development and education.* Washington, DC: National Association for the Education of Young Children.

Elkind, D. (2001). *The hurried child: Growing up too fast too soon.* Cambridge, MA: Perseus.

Emoto, M. (2006). *The secret of water for the children of the world.* Hillsboro, OR: Beyond Words.

Gardner, H. (1993). *Multiple intelligences: The theory in practice.* New York: Basic Books.

Gartell, D. J. (1994). *A guidance approach to discipline.* Albany, NY: Delmar.

Getskow, V., & Konczal, D. (1996). *Kids with special needs: Information and activities to promote awareness and understanding.* Santa Barbara, CA: The Learning Works.

Goleman, D. (1995). *Emotional intelligence: Why it can matter more than IQ.* New York: Bantam.

Gray, W. (1979). Understanding creative thought processes: An early formulation of the emotional-cognitive structure theory. *Man-Environment Systems 9*(1), 3–14.

Hannaford, C. (1995). *Smart moves: Why learning is not all in your head.* Arlington, VA: Great Ocean.

Hannaford, C. (2002). *Awakening the child heart: Handbook for global parenting.* Captain Cook, HI: Jamilla Nur.

Healy, J. M. (1999). *Endangered minds: Why children don't think and what we can do about it.* New York: Touchstone Books.

Heller, S. (2002). *Too loud, too bright, too fast, too tight: What to do if you are sensory defensive in an overstimulating world.* New York: HarperCollins.

Hubert, B. (2001). *Bal-A-Vis-X: Rhythmic balance/auditory/vision exercises for brain and brain-body integration.* Wichita, KS: Bal-A-Vis-X.

James, A. (2008). *School success for children with special needs: Everything you need to know to help your child learn.* San Francisco: Jossey-Bass.

Janke, R. A., & Peterson, J. P. (1995). *Peacemaker's A,B,Cs for young children: A guide for how to use the peace table.* Marine on St. Croix, MN: Growing Communities for Peace.

Jensen, E. (1998). *Teaching with the brain in mind.* Alexandria, VA: Association for Supervision and Curriculum Development.

Kagan, J. (1995). *The nature of the child.* New York: Basic Books.

Konner, M. (1991). *Childhood.* Boston: Little, Brown.

Kotulak, R. (1996). *Inside the brain: Revolutionary discoveries of how the mind works.* Kansas City, MO: Andrews and McMeel.

Lantieri, L. (Ed.). (2001). *Schools with spirit: Nurturing the inner lives of children and teachers.* Boston: Beacon.

Levine, M. (2002). *A mind at a time: America's top learning expert shows every child can succeed.* New York: Simon & Schuster.

MacClean, P. (1990). *The triune brain in evolution: Role in paleocerebral functioning.* New York: Plenum.

Moore, L. (2000). *Inclusion: A practical guide for parents: Tools to enhance your child's success in learning.* Thousand Oaks, CA: Corwin.

Moore, L. (2005). *Creating balance in children's lives: A natural approach to learning and behavior.* Thousand Oaks, CA: Corwin.

Moore, L., & Henrikson, P. (2005). *Creating balance in children: Activities to optimize learning and behavior.* Thousand Oaks, CA: Corwin.

Morris, L. R., & Schultz, L. (1989). *Creative play activities for children with disabilities: A resource book for teachers and parents* (2nd ed.). Champaign, IL: Human Kinetics.

Neugebauer, B. (Ed.). (1992). *Alike and different: Exploring our humanity with young children.* Washington, DC: National Association for the Education of Young Children.

Olson, S. A. (2001). *Tai chi for kids: Move with the animals.* Rochester, VT: Bear Cub Books.

Ostrander, S., & Schroeder, L. (with Ostrander, N.). (1994). *Superlearning 2000: New triple-fast ways you can learn, earn, and succeed in the 21st century.* New York: Delacorte.

Parette, H. P., Jr., Dunn, N. S., & Hoge, D. R. (1995). Low-cost communication devices for children with disabilities and their family members. *Young Children, 50*(6), 75–81.

Pearce, J. C. (1992). *Evolution's end: Claiming the potential of our intelligence.* San Francisco, CA: Harper.

Rapp, D. J. (1996). *Is this your child's world? How you can fix the schools and homes that are making your children sick.* New York: Bantam Books.

Ratey, J. J. (2001). *A user's guide to the brain: Perception, attention, and the four theaters of the brain.* New York: Pantheon Books.

Rich, D. (1992). *MegaSkills: In school and in life—The best gift you can give your child* (rev. ed.). Boston: Houghton Mifflin.

Schickedanz, J. (1999). *Much more than the a.b.c.'s: The early stages of reading and writing.* Washington, DC: National Association for the Education of Young Children.

Schlosser, E. (2002). *Fast food nation: The dark side of the all-American meal.* New York: HarperCollins.

Schwartz, S., & Miller, J. E. H. (1996). *The new language of toys: Teaching communication skills to children with special needs: A guide for parents and teachers.* Bethesda, MD: Woodbine House.

Sears, W., & Sears, M. (1999). *The family nutrition book: Everything you need to know about feeding your children from birth through adolescence.* Boston: Little, Brown.

Sears, W., & Sears, P. (with Foy, S.). (2003). *Dr. Sears' lean kids: A total health program for children ages 6–12.* New York: New American Library.

Siegel, L. M. (2007). *The complete IEP guide: How to advocate for your special ed child.* Berkeley, CA: Nolo.

Sobert, M. A., & Bogen, B. N. (1991). *Complete early childhood curriculum resource.* West Nyack, NY: The Center for Applied Research in Education.

Sousa, D. A. (2001). *How the brain learns: A classroom teacher's guide.* Thousand Oaks, CA: Corwin.

Sousa, D. A. (2001). *How the special needs brain learns.* Thousand Oaks, CA: Corwin.

Stordy, B. J., & Nicholl, M. J. (2000). *The LCP solution: The remarkable nutritional treatment for ADHD, dyslexia & dyspraxia.* New York: Ballantine.

Sumar, S. (1995). *Yoga for the special child: A therapeutic approach for infants and children with Down syndrome, cerebral palsy, and learning disabilities.* Buckingham, VA: Association for Supervision and Curriculum Development.

Sylwester, R. (1995). *A celebration of neurons: An educator's guide to the human brain.* Alexandria, VA: Association for Supervision and Curriculum Development.

U.S. Department of Education (2003). *Twenty-fifth annual report to Congress on the implementation of the Individuals with Disabilities Education Act.* Retrieved October 29, 2008, from http://www.ed.gov/about/reports/annual/osep/2003/index.html

Wise, A. (1995). *The high-performance mind: Mastering brainwaves for insight, healing, and creativity.* New York: Jeremy P. Tarcher/Putnam.

Wolery, M., & Wilbers, J. S. (Eds.). (1994). *Including children with special needs in early childhood programs.* Washington, DC: National Association for the Education of Young Children.

Wolfe, P. (2001). *Brain matters: Translating research into classroom practice.* Alexandria, VA: Association for Supervision and Curriculum Development.

Index